No Sweeter

NAME

40 Days to Discover the Wonder of the Name Above All Names

Richard W. LaFountain

Published by
Parakletos Press
Grove City, Pennsylvania
www.PrayerToday.org
Printed in the U.S.A.

ISBN (trade paper)
978-0-9858879-3-3

ISBN 978-0-9858879-3-3

51095>

9 780985 887933

All Scripture quotations, unless otherwise noted, are from the *King
James Version* of the Bible or are the author's own paraphrase.

Other Scripture portions are from the *Holy Bible, New International
Version® NIV®*, Copyright ©   1973, 1978, 1984 by International Bible
Society. Used by permission of Zondervan. All rights reserved

In Dedication

I dedicate this book to my mother, Phyllis June Belyea LaFountain, who led me to Jesus at an early age, and taught me through the Scriptures and by example to love Jesus with all my heart, mind, soul, and strength. She taught me to love that name and call on that name, whether for salvation, or in times of trouble, or for healing. Thank you mother for showing me Jesus. Now it's my turn to proclaim that *"name that is above every name,"* *"That whoever shall call on the name of the Lord will be saved."*

Jesus Is the Sweetest Name

There have been names that I have loved to hear,
But never has there been a name so dear
To this heart of mine, as the Name divine,
The precious, precious Name of Jesus.

Refrain
Jesus is the sweetest name I know,
And He's just the same as His lovely Name,
And that's the reason why I love Him so,"
Oh, Jesus is the sweetest name I know"

There is no name in earth or Heav'n above,
That we should give such honor and such love
As the blessed Name, let us all acclaim,
That wondrous, glorious Name of Jesus.

Refrain

And some day I shall see Him face to face
To thank and praise Him for His wondrous grace,
Which He gave to me, when He made me free,
The blessed Son of God called Jesus.

Preface

I have often preached on the names of the Lord. I believe if there were more preaching on Christ, his person and work, more people would be drawn to Jesus Christ. Jesus promised it, *"And I, if I be lifted up from the earth will draw all men unto myself."* (John 12:31) He was speaking of the cross but also of the exaltation of the message of the cross.

As the Apostle Paul said in Galatians 6:14 *"But God forbid that I should glory, save in the cross of our Lord Jesus Christ."*

The devotional book that you hold in your hand has been a long time in the making. It is the second devotional book I have written on the names of the Lord. The first, published in 2013, was a study of Old Testament names of the Lord in a 40-day devotional titled *Blessed Be the Name.* (Now available at www.PrayerToday.org and on Amazon.) This one is a 40-day look at the wonderful names of Jesus in the New Testament.

It is certainly not in any way an exhaustive study of the names, titles and descriptors of the Lord Jesus Christ. I began to write these devotionals based on some of my favorite names of Jesus in the New Testament. Then I found myself in the Gospel of John for over a year gleaning from the beloved disciple over 70 names, titles and descriptors of Jesus. That seemed much too long for a devotional, so I returned to my original intent to publish a few glimpses into the character and care of our Savior that might be helpful to us for daily living. His name is so great and inexpressible that only in heaven will we begin to really fathom the greatness of His person.

We have designed these devotionals to be easy glimpses into the rich character of Jesus through the kaleidoscope of His Word. For the average reader it is sufficient to read the Name, the explanation and the illustration of that name and apply to one's heart. For others with more time and curiosity we have designed discussion questions and a study guide for small groups. And for those with studious minds we suggest further word studies of the Name using Strong's Concordance, a topical study Bible such as Thompson's Chain Reference Bible, or Nave's Topical Bible.

Finally, we have provided a listing of wonderful hymns and songs that exalt the name of Jesus. We cannot print the lyrics here but provide the titles and authors so that you can do an Internet search to find the lyrics and listen to renditions of the songs on YouTube.

We encourage those studying in groups to download these tunes and lyrics to sing together and so join the myriad of saints and creatures before the throne of God who never cease to sing His praises.

Let's Study His Name

I have been studying, praying, meditating, writing and preaching on the Names of the Lord for a long time. There is nothing more stimulating to my soul and encouraging to my life and ministry than to fix my eyes on Jesus. I am waiting for the day he calls me home. In those first moments in heaven I won't care about the streets of gold, the heavenly music, or the friends and family reunited. My one supreme desire is to see my Savior face to face.

I have classified, collected, and culled over 700 names of Christ and God in the Scriptures. Many of them are metaphors or descriptions of his character and ministry, thus they are titles and not specific names. In this volume I have chosen 40 of my favorite names of the Lord to direct our attention over a 40-day period. Granted, these are but short vignettes or foretastes of who he is. To describe each in detail will take all eternity.

Through these meditations you will see the original Greek spellings of the names of the Lord. This to me is both helpful and insightful to see the original word that God used to describe himself or his Son.

Over the last 25 years I have embraced one of the names of the Lord each year to be my guide and fortress. It has been a rich experience of intimacy with God. If you choose to adopt a name of the Lord to carry with you during the year as I have done for many years, it will be helpful to have that name in the original as well as the English equivalent. You may want to print it out as a pictograph reminder of the Lord.

Deeper Study

You will also see strange numbers associated with the name. That number is from the *Strong's Concordance*. In 1890 James Strong, with the help of hundreds of scholars, wisely, helpfully, tediously and with great care catalogued all the words of the Bible in Hebrew or Greek and gave each one a number. (This was before computers or typewriters.) This has been immensely helpful for today's computer software programs that do Bible searches. The number you see in the index represents the Greek of that name as used in Scripture. For you and me that means we can track the occurrence of that particular word in the Bible, or in our case, a particular name used in the Bible and where it occurred. Thus I have included it here so you can continue to study and investigate the name for yourself.

My purpose in writing this devotional is to whet your appetite for the wonderful and multi-faceted Names of the Lord. May the Lord make himself near and dear to your heart as you pursue the matchless name of Jesus.

Our Study

Our present examination of the Names of the Lord will be in the format of a devotional book highlighting each of 40 names. One name each day will take you five weeks to cover all of the names. It can be used personally or corporately as a small group study. If you are pastor or a teacher you might consider doing a series on a group of those names.

Our study will include several features:

1. A Definition of that name according to the Word.
2. An Illustration from every day life
3. A Closing Thought and application of that name to your life.
4. A Prayer you might use in adopting that name.
5. A Study Guide of discussion questions for use in groups.
6. A Guide to Worship Songs on His Name.
7. A Word Study challenge to go deeper.

I have also included a list of 365 names organized topically into 52 weeks with seven names per week. Another list is available on my web site. It is my compiled list of 700 names gleaned over my years of study.

My hope is that this will inspire you to look into other Names of the Lord and make his name a life-long pursuit.

You can find these studies, and many more, in their entirety at www.PrayerToday.org

Uses for this Study

This is a 40 day devotional and study. We have chosen these 40 names as some of our favorites. Although we have archived 700 Names we have found in the Word, we present here 365 names organized by weeks of the year to whet your appetite for loving his names.

An Advent Exercise
We recommend it be used as a prelude to Christmas. Begin on or around November 15 through Christmas Day. Use it personally or as a family, carefully and prayerfully considering what Name the Lord himself will designate for you to carry with you into the coming year.

Study in Groups
This study equals almost six weeks of daily studies of the Name. Used weekly as a guide for small groups you have almost nine months of study, or three 13-week quarters and a few extra studies.

Memorization
We feel it is particularly important for the child of God, who carries the Name of the Lord in his heart and life, to commit to memory a key verse that speaks of that Name, and read or quote it every morning as you prepare for the day.

Deeper Study
We have included the *Strong's Concordance* number for the Hebrew Name so that you can search for it in the original language. But don't limit the scope of your deeper study to just the words used, follow the idea being conveyed in that word as well. Use *Nave's Topical Bible* or a similar topical reference Bible to track down the other references that may not use that word but convey the idea.

Exalt His Name Together
Many of the Names of the Lord can be represented in simple images and drawings. A sample of such images is given on our web site. Consider making Christmas tree ornaments with a Name of the Lord on each. Culminate your church participation in these 40 days with a Chrismon Service in which you decorate the tree with the Names of Christ. We have found this to be a highly anticipated and appreciated worship service prior to Christmas. A sample of such a service is given in this book.

Visualize the Name
Many items can be made that will remind you of his Name. By using either the Hebrew lettering, or any of the images, along with the key verse for the name, create a t-shirt with the Name, emblem, and/or proclamation of that Name. Make printed posters for your home or office with the Name and the verse as a daily reminder. Make a computer desktop wallpaper image with verse or image of the Name.

Experience more of

Jesus NAME

The Name of the Lord is an inexhaustible supply of strength and wisdom for the believer who is willing to seek his face. With over 700 names and titles of the Lord scattered throughout the Scriptures one will never exhaust the supply of names to explore and claim.

Dig Deeper

This devotional thought has just scratched the surface of the meaning and significance of this name. We have provided the Greek word for that name and the number of that word in *Strong's Concordance*. Another concordance provided on our web site at www.PrayerToday.org is a guide to a deeper understanding. Seek Him today!

Worship Him!

Knowing about the Lord's name is far different than knowing the Lord and worshiping his name. We have provided some helpful lists and links to worship music on YouTube and on our web site at www.PrayerToday.org that will help you exalt his name. Worship Him today!

Find More!

Now that you have tasted and found how good it is to know and claim the name of the Lord you are ready to explore some of his other wonderful names. We have provided a daily resource of 365 days each exalting a name of the Lord. As always, our web site www.PrayerToday.org is a place that is rich in resources and tools for prayer and magnifying the Name of the Lord.

Index of 40 New Testament Names

"The name of the Lord is a strong tower:
the righteous run into it and is safe." - Proverbs 18:10

The Name / Title	Verse	Strong's #	Greek
1. Abba Father	John 14:9	<5>	abba
2. Advocate	1 John 2:1	<3875>	parakletos
3. All in All	Colossians 3:11	<3956>	pas en pas
4. Alpha & Omega	Revelation 1:11	<01>	a - omega
5. Altar	Hebrews 13:10	<2379>	thusiasterion
6. Amen	Revelation 3:14	<281>	amen
7. Anchor	Hebrews 6:19	<45>	agkura
8. Author	Hebrews 5:9	<747>	archegos
9. Beginning/Ending	Revelation 1:8	<746>	arche
10. Bread	John 6:33-38	<740>	artos
11. Deliverer	John 8:32	<1658>	eleutheros
12. Doorway	Psalm 18:2	<2374>	thura
13. Friend	John 14:14	<5384>	philos
14. Gift	John 4:10	<1431>	dorea
15. Lamb	John 1:29	<286>	amnos
16. Resurrection	John 11:25	<386>	anastasis
17. Life	John 14:6	<222>	zoe
18. Light	John 8:12	<5457>	phos
19. Lion	Revelation 5:5	<30238>	leon
20. Morning Star	2 Peter 1:19	<3720>	aster
21. Physician	Luke 5:31	<2395>	iatros
22. Protector	John 17:11	<5083>	tereo
23. Rabboni	John 20:16	<4462>	rhabboni
24. Serpent	John 3:14-15	<3789>	ophis
25. Shepherd	John 10:11	<4166>	poimen
26. Truth	John 14:6	<225>	aletheia
27. Way	John 14:6	<3598>	hodos
28. Wing	Psalm 23:5	<4420>	pterux
29. Sanctifier	John 17:17-19	<37>	hagiazo
30. Finisher	Hebrews 12:2	<5051>	teleiotes
31. Vine	John 15:5	<288>	ampelos
32. Judge	2 Timothy 4:8	<2923>	krites
33. Word	John 1:1	<3056>	logos
34. Provider	Philippians 4:19	<4137>	pleroo
35. Potter	Romans 9:21	<2763>	kerameus
36. Ransom	1 Timothy 2:6	<487>	antilutron
37. I Am	John 8:58	<1510>	eimi
38. Bridegroom	John 3:29	<3566>	numphios
39. Jesus	Matthew 1:21	<2424>	Iesous
40. Almighty	Revelation 1:8	<3821>	pantokrator

Day 1
My "Abba" Father

*Don't you know me, Philip, even after I have been among you such a long time? Anyone who has seen me **has seen the Father**. How can you say, `Show us the Father'? -- John 14:9*

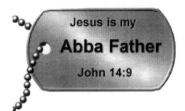

Many Christians did not have good fathers as a role model. Perhaps your dad was distant, unaffectionate, aloof, demanding, mean, cruel, or angry in words and actions. God knew that. God knew you would have a hard time relating to God the Father because of your broken father image. He knew you would feel rejected, judged, forsaken, and even unloved. He knew that was all you ever knew of a father's love. He knew before you were born that you would carry the scars of a marred relationship with your earthly father. So, God had a plan.

God's solution was to send Himself, disguised as his visible Son, to show His unfailing love and mercy to all His alienated children. Jesus is the Father disguised as the Son so that through him you might know the immensity of the Father's tender love.

The Apostle Paul said, *"In Him (Jesus) dwells all the fullness of the godhead bodily"* (Colossians 2:9) and *"He (Jesus) is the exact representation of His (God's) being."* (Hebrews 1:3) Phillip, one of Jesus' twelve disciples, pleaded, "Lord, show us the Father and we will be satisfied." Jesus was surprised and quick to respond, *"Don't you know me, Philip, even after I have been among you such a long time? Anyone who has seen me has seen the Father. How can you say, `Show us the Father'? Don't you believe that I am in the Father, and that the Father is in me? The words I say to you are not just my own. Rather, it is the Father, living in me, who is doing his work. Believe me when I say that I am in the Father and the Father is in me; or at least believe on the evidence of the miracles themselves."* (John 14:9-11) Thus Jesus was confirming what was written of Him in Isaiah 9:6, *"...he will be called Wonderful Counselor, Mighty God, Everlasting Father, Prince of Peace."*

The Hebrew word "Abba" is literally the word "Daddy." Jesus said, *"I will not leave you orphans (without a father), I will come to you."* (John 14:18) He was comforting the disciples that He was to them a Father and as such He would always be by their side, taking them by the hand, and helping them. (Isaiah 41:13) You are not an orphan! You are a child of the King. *He will never leave you nor forsake you.* (Hebrews 13:5)

Closing Thought

Many of us might have had poor or bad father examples. Many more in our day grow up without a father image at all. God wants to be your Father. He will stand by you and hold you by the hand saying, *"Do not be afraid. I am here. I will never leave you or forsake you."*

Prayer

Lord, I don't really know what it is to have a loving, caring father who picks me up in his arms and says, "I love you my child." Therefore, today, and for the rest of this year, I am asking you to be my Abba, FATHER. Show me your steadfast love. Take me by the hand and guide me. Hold me and never let me go. I ask this in Jesus' precious name, Amen.

Discuss Together

1. What is your best and favorite memory of your father?
2. What did you call your father? What was your relationship like?
3. Did any of you grow up without a father image in your home?
4. Who has been that father image to you in place of an earthly father?

Day 2
My Advocate

*If any man sin, we have an **advocate***
with the Father, Jesus Christ the righteous: -- 1 John 2:1

A few years ago our church faced a major lawsuit by a neighbor who resented that a church would be built in his community. So heated was the exchange that when I arrived at the township meeting, at which our zoning application would be discussed, there was standing room only.

As each of the evening's agenda items were clicked off it was narrowing down to us. One of the councilmen leaned over to me and said, "It looks like all these people are here to protest you!" And he was right.

The next day the Philadelphia Inquirer plastered my picture on the front page of the Neighborhood Section with an article to match. Needless to say we were in a pickle. We were within our rights to buy the property and build in the farmland area that was zoned for churches. Yet we felt like public enemy number one.

One of our church members suggested that we needed to retain an attorney to represent us. She also recommended that it be one that was well known by the judges, and other prosecutors in the county. So we did. We went straight to the top man with the most influence and retained his services.

That was the last township meeting I ever had to attend. Our attorney (our advocate) did the rest. He so intimidated the irate neighbor who himself was an attorney that the neighbor backed down and withdrew his complaint. Later we learned that he had incited the neighborhood against us under false pretenses. Eventually the opposition was dropped and the other neighbors all sent us letters of apology! It pays to have the right lawyer. Jesus is our attorney, our advocate who pleads our case before the Father.

Jesus stands before the throne of God and pleads our case before the Father. He is our defense attorney pleading the case that His blood cleanses us from all sin and therefore we stand complete in Him. He presents the evidence, we are sinners, but one paid for our sins who knew no sin that we might be made the righteousness of God.

Closing Thought

Many believers see Jesus as the prosecuting attorney rather than their defender. He does not accuse us before the Father. The enemy does that. He stands at our side before the throne of God and intercedes on our behalf. Your advocate makes a difference. He will make or break your case. Let Jesus represent you before the Father. He will plead your cause, then leave it in his capable hands and the results will be miraculous.

Prayer

Lord, I have to admit that I have often thought of you as my accuser when I sin. But now I realize that you do not accuse me in my sin, that's what the devil does. You are my defender, my advocate, my comforter to restore me and heal me, but never to condemn me. Thank you for your steadfast love that never fails, even when I fail you.

Discuss Together

1. Have you ever been sued? Share the situation and how you felt when you first were informed that you were being sued.
2. Have you ever been accused of a crime, or perhaps gone to court to plead your cause over a traffic ticket? Share your story.
3. I am sure some lawyer jokes would be appropriate at this point. Why do you think we even have so many lawyer jokes? What are lawyers known for?

Day 3
My All, and In All

*There is neither Greek nor Jew, circumcision nor uncircumcision, Barbarian, Scythian, bond nor free: but Christ is **all, and in all**.*
-- Colossians 3:11

Paul's letter to the Colossians is filled with references to the supremacy and preeminence of Christ, not only in the believer's life but in the universe. The terms "All in all" and "All and in all" are continual themes in Paul's writings. Paul was obsessed with Jesus. His stated purpose in life was to know him in the power of his resurrection. Now he wants believers everywhere to have this same fixation on Jesus Christ that he be everything to them, in life and in death

I remember watching Popeye cartoons and the Three Stooges. It seems we were too often in front of the old black and white dimly lit TV watching silly cartoons. There is not much of redemptive value in those comedic routines, but once in a while a glimmer of truth seeped through. Popeye was my favorite. I remember several quotes from that spinach satrap. One was this, "I am what I am, and that's all that I am."

The idea was you are whatever you are, so deal with it. You have to get up in the morning, every morning, and look in the mirror, so you'd better get used to it. You are what you are, and there is no changing that. We just need to deal with the fact that we are flawed and weak.

Paul reiterates for God's people that we are what we are and there is no changing that. One recurring theme in Colossians is that in Christ dwelt all the fullness of the godhead bodily. (Col. 1:15-17, 2:3, 2:9-10, 2:19, and 3:10) Paul exhorts and encourages us, who might be feeling that we were given a raw deal or dealt a bad hand. He reiterates Christ is in everything, including your lot in life.

We were created by him and for him. He knows our name and our frame. (Ps. 139:14) Therefore, whatever our lot, like it or not, whether Greek, Jew, circumcised, uncircumcised, barbarian, Scythian, bond or free, male or female, smart or not so smart, pretty or homely, tall or short, fat or skinny, lucky or unlucky, God is in all of it. Christ is ALL and IN ALL. He planned it that way for his glory and your good.

Closing Thought

Fundamentally, this means that Jesus is everything I need. He is my All and in All. He is EVERYTHING to me. There is nothing, and no one, more important than Jesus Christ. Is that true for you today? Is He your all in all, or maybe your half and half, or perhaps He's just your 2%? Today He wants to be 100% to you and have 100% of you. "Not just a part, nor half of my heart. I will give ALL to Thee."

Prayer

Lord, I have a lot of things I've been clinging to as my security blanket. You are the only thing of true value and worth. Let me always trust you as my All in All. My hardest battle is to trust that you are "in" everything, whether it be good, bad, or ugly. Help me to see you as "IN" my circumstances. Then I can truly give you thanks *"in everything, [knowing] this is the will of God in Christ Jesus concerning me."*

Discuss Together:

1. After you have looked up and read together the above passages consider how great Jesus is. Can you use any superlative of him that is not true? Can you possibly exaggerate his greatness?
2. Can you think of other hymns, songs and choruses that exalt Jesus? Sing them together as an expression of Christ being your all in all.
3. Believers should be braggers about Jesus. Paul said, "Let him that glories (brags) glory in the Lord." Spend some time glorying in the Lord's person and greatness by sharing what he means to you

Day 4
My Alpha and Omega

*I am **Alpha and Omega**, the first and the last: -- Revelation 1:11*

The Alpha Male: Dogs and wolves show deference to the alpha male in their pack by allowing them to be the first to eat. The alpha can be male or female. Wolves use eye contact as an indicator of dominance or submission, but in order to establish a dominant position they often also show physical superiority through playing or

fighting. This is true for most social animals, including chimpanzees and man. Social dominance and the "pecking order" begins early in life

Directly related to the preeminence of Christ is the description that He is the Alpha and the Omega, the beginning and the ending, the first and the last. It is no accident that Jesus appears in the last book of the bible, Revelation, as the Alpha and Omega. Genesis starts with *"In the beginning God"* and Revelation ends with *"the Omega, the last, the ending."*

"Alpha: is the first letter of the Greek alphabet. **"Omega"** is the last letter. We even derive our word for letters from the Greek "alpha" when we say "alphabet." The English equivalent of this name is God saying I am "A" and "Z." The clarifier is always the accompanying statement that I am the first and the last, the beginning and the ending.

Hebrews 1 describes Jesus as the Creator, as from the beginning, imperishable, and as never-ending. The earth however, and all things and people in it grow old, and like a garment wear out. God, however, does not wear out. He does not grow old. He really has no beginning or ending in himself. He always was and always will be. Yet for us he is our Alpha and Omega. That is, He is our beginning and ending. He is the starter and finisher of all things. Nothing starts without Him and nothing ends without Him. He is the Boss from start to finish.

Paul declares, *"He is before all things and by him all things hold together. He is the head, the first born, so that in everything he has the supremacy."* (Colossians 1:15-18) God wants us to know that he is the first cause and the last cause.

Closing Thought

We can know and be assured that if anything good is going to happen in us, to us, by us, it will be because the Alpha and Omega, the starter and ender of all things determines it to be so. All good comes from him. He is the Author and Finisher, the Alpha and Omega, the Beginning and Ending, the First and the Last. This world is not about you. It is about the Lord. He wants to have preeminence in everything. (Colossians 1:18) He who began creation with His First Word will have the Last Word. He is the Alpha and the Omega, the Beginning and Ending, the First and the Last.

Prayer

Lord, You are the A-Z in my life. You have been writing my starts and finishes throughout my days. Therefore today, I give You all the A-Z's in my life. I give You the things I can't figure out. I give You the bad things that look like disasters to me. I give You the little things and the big things. Because it all belongs to You and You are working it together for Your glory and my good. Thank you, Lord!

Discuss Together

1. Who is the alpha male in your life? Who's the boss? Who is the dominant person? Who rules your roost?
2. Can other persons or things be so dominant in our hearts and lives that it robs Jesus of his rightful place as Alpha and Omega? What kinds of things compete with the Lordship of Christ in your life?
3. What do you know about the preexistence of Christ? Can you show us that Christ was Alpha, that is, first created before the world began? Where? Is that an important issue to our faith?

Day 5
My Altar

*We have an **altar**, whereof they have no right to eat.* -- Hebrews 13:10

Altars aren't used much anymore. When I was growing up we had what Mom called, Family Altar. By that she meant we all gathered in our living room for a sacred time of Scripture reading and prayer every day.

In the church where I was raised the altar was a kneeling step and rail in front of the platform. As I child I always thought it was a barricade to keep people from getting to the preacher. The church altar was often used at the end of the service as a place of repentance and surrender. It was a place to get right with God. It was a place to surrender yourself totally to the Lord.

Recently in the little church where I served as an interim pastor there was a great upheaval about someone removing the huge pulpit furniture, three platform chairs, and the old wooden altar from in front of the church to make room for musical instruments. It wasn't so much that they wanted to use the altar, it was just one of those many "sacred cows" we cling to because it was a tradition. Someone wisely argued against keeping them when he said, "Why do you care? You never use it anyway."

The altar in both Old and New Testaments meant a place where people went to meet God or offer sacrifices to God, but much more than that it was a place of cleansing. Noah was the first to be mentioned as building an altar to the Lord where he offered sacrifices of thanksgiving after the flood. In the Old Testament sense the altar was a place to remember where something great happened in your relationship with God, so one built an altar as a memorial of that important event.

In Isaiah 6 the prophet saw the Lord high and lifted up and his train filling the temple. Feeling his sinful unworthiness before God, an angel took a coal from off the altar in heaven, placed it on his tongue, and declared him clean. The altar is where we go to be purified, cleansed, and forgiven. Jesus is our altar. He is where we go to be cleansed and forgiven. The sacrifice is not ours to give. He already gave the ultimate sacrifice once for all when he laid down his body on the altar of sacrifice for us.

Closing Thought

If God provided an altar in heaven, isn't it logical that we would need one on earth too? That altar is at the feet of Jesus. You want cleansing? Come to Jesus. You need to surrender something back to God? Come to Jesus. You need to pray something through? Come to Jesus. He is our altar, and the altar always says, "Come, this is the meeting place of God. This is where you do business with God."

Prayer

Lord, I have failed to come to you as often as I should when I am in need. I am often too busy or too harassed to take time to kneel quietly by my bedside or at a chair to seek your help and blessing. Teach me Lord to recognize that you are my altar by physically bowing before you and surrendering my need.

Discuss Together

1. Does your church have an altar? What is it used for?
2. Do you have any memorial altars where you did business with God?
3. Have you, or anyone you've known, obeyed Matthew 5:23 *"leave your gift at the altar and be restored first."*?
4. Is there anything in your life that needs to be placed on the altar?

Day 6
My Amen

*These things says the **Amen**, the faithful and true witness, the beginning of the creation of God; -- Revelation 3:14*

The word "Amen" is not unfamiliar to us even in a post Christian world. Amen is what we say at the end of a prayer. For most of us it means the end, the finish of a prayer or a worship service. For others it is a word of agreement to something that has been spoken. The preacher makes a  good stirring point and people used to say a hearty "Amen!" Today they may just nod their heads or mumble a "right on."

This Hebrew word means "<u>firm</u>", and hence also faithful. In Isaiah 65:16 the Authorized Version has "*the God of Truth,*" which in Hebrew is "*the God of Amen.*" It is frequently used by our Savior to give emphasis to his words where it is translated "verily." Sometimes, however, in John's Gospel, it is repeated, "Verily, verily."

Strong's Concordance explains it this way:
> *"The word "amen" is a most remarkable word. It was transliterated directly from the Hebrew into the Greek of the New Testament, then into Latin and into English and many other languages, so that it is practically a universal word. It has been called the best known word in human speech. The word is directly related--in fact, almost identical --to the Hebrew word for "believe" (amam), or faithful. Thus, it came to mean "sure" or "truly", an expression of absolute trust and confidence."*

The Amen was used at the end of a statement meaning ""So be it, or "may it be fulfilled." It was a custom which passed over from the synagogues to the Christian churches, that when the one who had read the Scriptures or spoken and prayed, the others responded, Amen, and thus they made the substance of what was uttered their own.

"Amen" is not supposed to be the last word, but the absolute word. It means an "absolute certainty." Today people often say "absolutely" in agreement with something they are talking about. They mean yes, an unequivocal "YES." Jesus is our absolute certainty. There is no variableness in him, no shadow of turning. He is the same yesterday, today and forever. He is the absolute truth. He is the faithful and true witness. It is used as a title of the Lord Jesus Christ by the Apostle John in Revelation 3:14.

Closing Thought

Amen means "It's a done deal!" It's an emphatic firm foot-stomped-on-the-ground absolute unchanging truth. It ought to so catch a hold of us that our hearts burn within us like an exploding volcano that we can't hold it in any longer, and we burst forth with a loud audible "YES!" – "AMEN!"

Prayer

Lord, I admit that I have not been comfortable saying "Amen" much less shouting "AMEN!" Help me to so believe your absolute truths that it will stir me deep inside to thrill at the victory of my Savior over all the powers of hell enough to unashamedly shout a loud, "AMEN!" and not care who hears it.

Discuss Together

1. Is there anyone in your church who often says a loud AMEN or HALLELUJAH? How does it make you feel when they do that?
2. Is it necessary or useful for Christians to say a loud "Amen" in church services?
3. When is the most appropriate place to say a loud "Amen"?
4. When is the last time you burst forth with an unprompted "Amen!" when Jesus is exalted?

Day 7
My Anchor

*Which hope we have as an **anchor** of the soul, both sure and steadfast, and which enters into that within the veil; -- Hebrews 6:19*

My Anchor

Hebrews 6:19

Anchors are essential to ships and boats. Without them any sea vessel will be carried to and fro by the winds of passing storms. Christ, as our Anchor, affirms two realities 1) There will be storms that come into all of our lives regardless of the size of our boat. 2) We will all need something solid and immovable to cling to when those inevitable storms come.

Anchors have slowly evolved through the centuries, but the principle of the anchor is always the same. An anchor is a heavy weight that remains on the sea bottom in a stationary position, while the wind beats relentlessly at the ship above. The earliest anchors were rocks heavy enough to hold a ship in place during a storm. Today many anchors are made of a heavy iron weight with arms, called flukes, that turn and grip the sandy sea bottom or snag rocks or coral on the sea bed. The best anchors, however, are found in safe havens or harbors where the ship can be anchored, or moored, to an immovable rock. That is called a permanent mooring.

This permanent mooring is what the author of Hebrews was referring to when he spoke of an anchor "that is sure and steadfast." It is an anchor that is tethered to something immovable and permanent. What is immovable? The answer is found in the same book of Hebrews. In Hebrews 13:8 it says that *"Jesus Christ is the same, yesterday, today and forever."* And in Hebrews 11:6 it says that his promises are the chains that tether us to the Immovable One, our rock. Just as Jesus is permanent, unmovable and changeless, so are his promises. It is in this context that our key verse regarding "an anchor" appears. He says that by two immutable things we can be sure. The first is that God swore on an oath, and the second is that it is impossible for God to lie. Therefore we have strong consolation and a sure hope. Think of His promises as the chain that connects the anchor to the boat.

Closing Thought
God Himself is Our Faithful Unchanging Anchor. Here are a few anchors for your soul.

1. **God loves you & has a plan for your life. Jeremiah 29:11, Rom 8:35-39**
2. **God cares about you. Matthew 6:26**
3. **God answers prayer. Matthew 18:18-20**
4. **God forgives you all your iniquities. Psalm 103:3**
5. **God works everything out for your good and his glory. Romans 8:28**
6. **God will supply all your needs. Philippians 4:19**
7. **God is able to make all grace abound to you. 2 Corinthians 9:8**
8. **God is able to do immeasurably more... Eph. 3:20**

Prayer
Lord, help me to hang on to my Anchor. You aren't affected by the storms that swirl around me. Jesus, even you fell asleep in a storm at sea because you had absolute trust that your Father was the Anchor and kept you from sinking. Help me to be able to rest in your unfailing love and care today.

Discuss Together
1. Have you ever been in a storm at sea? Describe your adventure.
2. Have you ever been sea sick? Share your experience.
3. What might be the storms of life that require an anchor?
4. What does it mean to be "tossed to and fro." (Is. 54:11, Eph 4:14, James 1:6)
5. What is the hardest storm you've ever faced in your spiritual life?
6. How might you find Jesus' title, "Anchor of the Soul," a name that carries you through the coming year?
7. Choose at least 10 sure promises from God that you will tether your heart to this year. Why these? Share them with each other.

Day 8
My Author

*And being made perfect, he became the **author***
of eternal salvation unto all them that obey him; -- Hebrews 5:9

You are sitting in an English class for a final exam. The professor places before you a blank sheet of paper and says you have two hours to write a short story. What do you write? The sheet of paper is blank. The possibilities are as limitless as Webster's Dictionary. All you have to do is arrange those 162,000 words in the American dictionary into intelligible sentences and paragraphs to make a non-existent story come to life. In theology we call that "*Creatio ex nihilo*" ('creation out of nothing'). That is how God created the world.

He is the author of all things. He is the first cause, the starter, and the finisher of everything that exists. All that exists in creation existed first in the mind of God, then he commanded it into existence. The story of life and creation goes as he dictates. The story does not unravel itself with a life of its own. There is no such thing as evolution or destiny apart from his design. He is the author. Without him there is no story. It is his story. He is the sole author

The characters in the story don't create the story or do whatever they want. They do what the author dictates. They do not create their own adventures. They depend on the author. He writes the story. They are the actors. It is the author who chooses the characters, their looks, the scenes, the storyline, their adventures, their costumes, and their personalities; he guides even their dialogue. He is the author of all things. When he says the story is over, it is over.

When God calls himself the author and finisher of our faith he means he is sovereign over all. He creates, he decides, he ordains, he chooses, he leads, he directs, and he orchestrates. Nothing is left to chance!

There is great value in knowing that the Lord is Author and Finisher. It is not up to our own efforts or devices. *"It is God who works in you to will and do his good pleasure."* (Philippians 2:13) We have a humorous adage, "It is not over until the fat lady sings," referring to the closing of an opera. Yet, the truth is, "It is not over until the Author says it is over."

Closing Thought

Do you need someone to rewrite your story? I know the Author and He is able to do immeasurably more than we ask or even imagine. He has a story in mind for you since the foundation of the world. Invite him today to begin rewriting "the rest of the story."

Prayer

O Lord, I see from this verse that you are the author of my story. You are not making it up as you go. You have a plan. You made me your character for the glory of your story. As my personal story unfolds help me not to become fearful that the story won't end well. *"For I know that all things work together for the good of them that love you, who are called according to your purpose."*

Discuss Together

1. What is your favorite novel, book, or short story?
2. If you could rewrite your life story, what would you write? How would you change it? How would it end?
3. Read Jeremiah 29:11 and discuss God's plans and dreams for your ideal life. What would that look like?

Day 9
My Beginning and Ending

*I am Alpha and Omega, the **beginning** and the ending, says the Lord, which is, and which was, and which is to come, the Almighty.*
-- Revelation 1:8

Jesus is the beginning of everything. John says that nothing that was made was made except by him. Before the earth was fully created Jesus spoke the world into existence. By his word the worlds were made, the stars were put into place, planets began to march around the sun, and the universe came into existence in a moment. He is the initiator of all that we know and have ever experienced. In fact, John says he has life and is the author of all life. (John 1:1-2) As the Father has life in himself so the Son has life in himself and to whomever he gives it. (John 5:26) Everything that exists, tangible or intangible, living or inanimate was made by him and for him. (Colossians 1:16)

He is the beginning.
He is the starting place. He jump started everything in the universe. Nothing happens without him initiating it. He knows the end from the beginning and everything in between. He is like a perfect circle, having neither beginning or ending, but yet it has a beginning and a place to end. Everything starts with him and ends with him.

Both John and Paul say our life began when Jesus came in. John says, *"You must be born again,"* that means we must be born from above. (John 3:3)   We all are dead ending to eternal death until we get a new start. Jesus is the place of new beginnings. We are born again by the living Word of God, Jesus, the word of God that lives and abides forever. (1 Peter 1:23) John says in 1 John 5:12, *"He that has the son has life and he that has not the Son of God has not life."* That puts it pretty clearly. Life begins with Jesus.

The Apostle Paul says He (Jesus) makes everything new. He makes us new creatures, new people with a new heart and life. *"Therefore if any man be in Christ, he is a new creature: old things are passed away; behold, all things are become new."* (2 Corinthians 5:17) He also includes wonderful faith-filled promises from the "Do-Over King." *"He that began a good work in you will perform it unto the day of Jesus Christ."* (Philippians 1:6)

27

Closing Thought

Do you need a fresh start? Ask Jesus. He came to give you a new beginning. He spoke the world into existence without anything else. He can and will speak the word and call your new life into existence too. "Oh," you say, "I have a new life in Christ but I've messed it up. I've ruined that new life." Then call on him. He will make you over anew.

Prayer

Lord, there are days when I wish I could just start all over again, erase the past, forget the mistakes, clean the slate, and begin all over again. I know I can't do that, but You can. You are the beginning of everything. Be my new beginning. Your word says, *"Your mercies are new every morning."* Let every day with you be a new beginning for me.

Discuss Together

1. Share your personal testimony of a new start, your new beginning with Jesus.
2. Share some personal experience of your own failure or sin when God gave you a new start, a do-over. It's not easy to be transparent, but remember we are all sinners, saved by grace. Hiding our sin or pretending we were never sinners isn't helpful. It's hypocrisy. Be transparent.
3. Jesus is the starting place for all new things. Consider together all the people Jesus encountered, how many of them had new beginnings out of bad starts? (Mary Magdalene, Lazarus, Matthew, etc.)

Day 10
My Daily Bread

*I am the **bread of life**. He who comes to me will never go hungry, and he who believes in me will never be thirsty.* -- John 6:33-38

My Daily Bread

John 6:33

I'm not crazy about American over-processed bread. It's OK, but it's not great. Growing up in the Midwest I knew only packaged bread and the occasional homemade bread my mother would make. I can't say that I've ever craved bread, maybe toast, but not just plain old white bread.

It wasn't until we served as missionaries in Brazil that we learned what "real" bread tasted like. Now, that's good bread. It is made fresh a couple times a day at a bakery. Brazilians have fresh bread for breakfast, and then later in the afternoon at the coffee hour they have more fresh bread. It's light, fresh and delicious. You don't want to eat day old bread though. It's not nearly as tasty. Nothing smells so good and tastes so great as fresh Brazilian bread. It makes my mouth water just thinking about it.

The Jews of Jesus' day knew about the amazing bread called manna that came down from heaven six days a week for over forty years in the wilderness in the time of Moses. That manna spoiled if it were kept overnight, except on the Sabbath when it miraculously stayed fresh for two days. Each morning the people of Israel would go out and find it on the ground. That manna stopped after they entered the Promise Land, but a sample of it was stored in the Ark of the Covenant and secreted away by Jeremiah before the fall of Jerusalem. The Jews believed that when the Messiah would come he would open the ark and provide them with this everlasting bread from heaven. You see, the Jews of Jesus' day had never seen nor tasted real manna. They heard about it. They craved it. They dreamed of it. They thought it was super bread (Ex 16:4, Ps 78:24) that brought health and long life. It was angel's food.

When Jesus said, "I am the Bread of Life", it was in the context of having fed 5,000 men, plus women and children with five small loaves and two tiny fish. Jesus was responding to the people's craving for manna from heaven. Then Jesus clarified, *"I am the bread that came down from heaven."* (John 6:42) He did not say he came to give them manna, but that he was the manna from heaven that God sent to them. Jesus is THE BREAD of Life. We are to daily feed on Him through His Word.

Closing Thought

How often we are just like that. We don't really want Jesus. We want what Jesus can get us. We want health and wealth. We want Jesus to meet our needs, heal our bodies, fill our bank accounts, keep us safe from harm, and give us a happy life. We don't really want Jesus. We want what Jesus provides for us. We are consumers. What we crave says a lot about us. What are you craving, pining after, dreaming about, searching for?

Prayer

Lord, I don't always crave you. I live on earth and my desires are predominantly earthly. I'm like the people around me. I live for daily bread. I live to make a living, provide for my family, and accumulate a few good things in this life. That seems to take up so much of my time that I don't have much time left for you. Teach me to crave the things of the Word that are good for me, not just the sugar coated stuff, but the real hefty meaty stuff. Teach me to hunger for you.

Discuss Together

1. Do you have any fond memories of grandma's house and some of the great food smells that emanated from the kitchen? What were your favorite smells? Foods? Do you remember fresh bread being baked?
2. What's your favorite food in all the world? If you had to subsist on just one food, what would it be? Do you think you'd get tired of it?
3. Discuss the story of manna. (Exodus 16, Numbers 16:31) What do you think manna looked like? Tasted like? Would you be content to have manna for 40 years?
4. Discuss Hebrews 5:12-14 where Paul talks to saints about milk and meat. What do you think the milk of the Word is? What would the bread of the Word be? What would strong meat be?

Day 11
My Deliverer

*Then you will know the truth, and the truth will **set you free**...*
*So if the Son sets you free, you will be **free indeed**.* -- John 8:32-36

Most of us have never experienced slavery firsthand. It is a far off concept that unfortunate people suffered centuries ago. Perhaps the closest thing to slavery experienced in our day is being a prisoner of war.

Louis Zamperini was a real life hero portrayed in the recent movie, "*Unbroken*." His story is worth reading by every Christian because it is not just a story of being a prisoner of war but also of becoming a prisoner of alcohol and anger and being set free by Jesus.

Louis was an aviator whose plane crashed while on a search and rescue mission on May 27, 1943 during WWII. He drifted 47 days in the Pacific Ocean with his fellow airmen dying of hunger and thirst. They were picked up by a Japanese ship and taken to a prison camp in Japan where he was tortured incessantly until the end of the war when he and his fellow prisoners were rescued. Throughout his prison experience he was singled out for the harshest treatment because he had been an Olympic star. It is a sad tale of life without hope in isolation and constant pain and suffering. Zamperini eventually survived the horrors of the Japanese prison camp and was rescued and returned to the States only to become a prisoner to alcohol and his own anger toward the cruel prison guard who caused him so much suffering.

Zamperini was a slave in prison until he was rescued by the American air force. Then he was a slave of sin until one night in a Billy Graham Crusade he walked forward to receive Jesus Christ as his personal Lord and Savior. That night his entire life changed as the chains of alcohol and hatred fell off at the foot of the cross.

Though none of us may ever have to go through the terrible ordeal of being a prisoner and slave of a foreign enemy, yet we all experience varying degrees of slavery to sin. Jesus came to destroy the work of the devil and set us free from the prison house of our own sinful nature. He is our Deliverer.

Closing Thoughts

Sin, any sin, is like quicksand. Once you step into it you're trapped by the downward pull of it. The only hope of escape is for someone to pull you free. Jesus is our deliverer, our liberator, the only one who can set us free. Call on him.

Prayer

Lord, I'm so stupid. I know sin is a trap, but sometimes I think it won't get me, and I can get out of any trouble I might get into – but then I get stuck. It's like my truck gets stuck in the muck and I just spin my wheels. The harder I try the deeper I go. Lord, have mercy on me. Rescue me. Take my hand, pull me out. Set me free.

Discuss Together

1. Not many of us have ever been in prison but if you have, describe what it was like.
2. Perhaps you've read a biography or autobiography of someone who was locked away in a terrible prison. Share what you remember of their misery.
3. John Bunyan in Pilgrim's Progress describes the Dungeon of Despair. Find a copy and read from that section describing the prison house.
4. Look up a description of London's Newgate prison and share with others the horrors of being incarcerated there in the 12th to 16th centuries.
5. If you have ever read the book or seen the movie *Roots* by Alex Haley, you will find some pretty graphic descriptions of slavery and the suffering they endured in the holds of ships on their journey to America. Share your discoveries.

Day 12
My Doorway

*I am **the door** by me if any man enter in, he shall be saved; and shall go in and out, and find pasture. -- John 10:9*

Doors are good. Without them everything would be open for burglars to walk in and steal your goods. With Shepherds doors were not wooden openings, they weren't even gates that swing. This door of which Jesus spoke was a living door. Shepherds in the time of Jesus did not have fenced in corrals for the sheep. Instead the shepherd would lead them to an area closed in by rocks and he would place himself at the only opening and act as a door. No one came in or out except by his permission. He was the door. There was only one way into that sheepfold. It was through him. One day that door will close once and for all. The day you die and enter into eternity the door will be permanently shut. (Rev 21) Will you be on the inside or the outside? There is another door Jesus refers to in Revelation 3.20. It is the door of your heart and life. *"Behold I stand at the door and knock, if any man hear my voice and open the door, I will come in to him, and dine with him, and he with me."*

While serving as missionaries in Brazil we were led to do an outdoor children's puppet theater in the parks as a means to reach children and adults with the message of Jesus. We did humorous puppet skits, games, songs and a Bible story. One of the songs we taught to the children was based on Revelation 3.20 where Jesus said, *"I stand at the door and knock."* Years later a parent told us that she was listening each week from the balcony of her apartment and said that that song made her mad. She didn't like being told she was on the outside of the door looking in, but her heart longed to enter in and be saved. Eventually she made her way down to the park to stand with us and there she opened her heart's door and let Jesus come in.

Jesus is Knocking. Will you answer? *"Behold, I stand at the door, and knock: if any man hear my voice, and open the door, I will come in to him, and will sup with him, and he with me."*
(Revelation 3:20)

Closing Thoughts

Jesus is the door or gate to the sheepfold. The sheepfold is the family of God. There is no other way to enter into the Kingdom of God and God's family but by becoming a child of God through faith in the Lord Jesus Christ. He is the door by which you may enter and receive everlasting life. His door will open when you call on his name. The other door is the door of your heart. If you close out Jesus he will stay just where he is and has been, knocking at your heart's door seeking to gain entrance. Is your door shut or open?

Prayer

Lord Jesus, I realize that I have always loved you and admired you. But today I realize that I have left you waiting outside of my heart and life. I have never really asked you to come into my life. Today Lord, the door is open and I invite you to come into my heart to forgive my sin and make me your child.

Discuss Together

1. Did you ever get locked out of your house or car? Tell us about that experience. How did you feel? What did you do? How did you get in?
2. Have you ever had a burglar break into your home? Were your doors locked? Were you there? If you were there what would you have done?
3. Did you ever sell anything door to door? Did you ever have a door slammed in your face? How did it make you feel?

Day 13
My Friend

*Greater love has no one than this that he lay down his life for his **friends**. You are **my friends** if you do what I command I no longer call you servants, because a servant does not know his master's business. Instead; I have called you **friends**.* -- John 15:14

My Friend

John 15:14

Everyone wants and needs a true friend. But perhaps you've been jilted or betrayed by a friend. You pretend to be autonomous and you don't need a friend. Real friends are hard to come by. They aren't just colleagues, acquaintances, or people you like to be with. A true friend is characterized by love, not by like. A friend loves at all times. By love I mean a tenacious, unassailable, non-vacillating, changeless, steadfast commitment, not just to endure you, but to love you through thick and thin. A fair weather friend is not a friend.

Jesus declared himself to be a friend to his disciples. He was a friend, not a colleague, a boss, a slave driver, a teacher, teammate, or coach. His commitment to them was to love them no matter what the cost. In fact, all his friends abandoned him at his arrest, but he continued to love them. John says, *"Greater love than this no man has ever shown, that a man would lay down his life for his friends."* Jesus laid down his life for us to make us his friends. That commitment was a love sealed by blood. The disciples didn't deserve it. They didn't earn it. But he loved them anyway. The disciples weren't good friends. They were unreliable. They ran away in adversity. They even denied knowing him. But Jesus is the friend of the friendless.

Many of us have a hard time with friendships, yet everybody longs to have a good friend. Wendy Francisco is a dog lover and a musician. She cleverly put together a cute song or ballad that compares the loyal friendship of a dog to the steadfast love of the Father. It is not meant to compare God to a dog, but to remind us that God put animals in the world to describe to us His own invisible personality trait. The dog is a great God-given illustration of God's never-failing love. You can see that song on the next page, and if you go to Wendy's web site you can hear her sing it. Give it a listen.

Closing Thought
You may be a lousy friend. You've got good company. But aren't you glad that God knows that? So he sent us a FAITHFUL BEST FRIEND who will never let God down and will never let you down. Paul says, *"If we are faithless, he will remain faithful, for he cannot*

disown himself." (2 Timothy 2:13) Jesus is our faithful friend who laid down his life for us. *"What, then, shall we say in response to this? If God is for us, who can be against us? He who did not spare his own Son, but gave him up for us all--how will he not also, along with him, graciously give us all things?"* (Romans 8:31-32)

Prayer
0 Lord, I'm so ashamed. I am not a faithful friend. I have failed you many times over. I have failed those I call my friends. But I thank you that you are the perfect friend at all times. You love me no matter what and you already proved your love for me when you laid down your life on the cross. May I be called a "friend of God" not because of me, but because of You.

Discuss Together
1. Who is your very best friend of all time? What made you best friends? Share your experience with best friends.
2. Can you name a friend who was there for you when you were down and hurting? Do you have any friends that can say anything and tell you the truth even when it hurts?

GoD and DoG
by Wendy Francisco

I look up and I see GoD.
I look down and see my dog.
Simple spelling G O D,
Same word backwards, D O G.

They would stay with me all day.
I'm the one who walks away.
But both of them just wait for me,
and dance at my return with glee.

Both love me no matter what,
divine God and canine mutt.
I take it hard each time I fail,
but God forgives, Dog wags his tail.

God thought up and made the dog,
dog reflects a part of God.
I've seen love from both sides now,
it's everywhere, amen, bow wow.

I look up and I see God,
I look down and see my dog
And in my human frailty,
I can't match their love for me.

© 2009 Crack O'Noon Music
http://godanddog.org

36

Day 14
My Indescribable Gift

*If you knew **the gift of God** and who it is that asks you for a drink,*
you would have asked him and he would have given you living water.
-- John 4:10

People give gifts of all kinds of sizes and values to express their love and affection. Here are a few gifts highlighted this year in several magazines that searched the globe for the most expensive and most impressive gifts you can give someone at Christmas, or any other occasion.

- A Bodycast of Muhammad Ali – Price: $15 Million
- 1964 Ferrari 250 LM – Price: $12 million to $15 million
- Dolce & Gabbana's DG2027B Sunglasses – Price: $383,609
- Heels By Christopher Michael Shellis – Price: $218,407
- Virgin Galactic Space Trip – Price: $250,000
- Signed copy of Birds of America – Price: $165,000
- Zafirro Razor – Price: $100,000
- Fonderie 47 Cufflinks – Price: $32,659
- Gold Shoelaces By Mr. Kennedy – Price: $19,000
- Nate Lowman Converse Sneakers – Price: $25,000
- A Savannah Cat – Price: $12,000-$35,000

Those might be unusual and highly expensive gifts, but they are silly gifts. They will soon be used up, rusted, outdated, and may even become useless. But God's gift is an everlasting gift that is so rich, so beyond description it is called an unspeakable gift. Jesus is the gift of God.

Jesus said an extraordinary thing. *"If you knew the gift of God and who it is that asks you."* What is the gift of God? The gift of God according to the Bible is multifaceted; like a diamond it has many faces but is part of the whole.

This woman Jesus was speaking to was a sinner. She had five husbands and was living with another who wasn't her husband. That's amazing. She was a young woman, probably quite attractive and seductive. How do you go through five husbands before you are thirty and you're working on a sixth? But Jesus was there trying to straighten out her sex life, or fix her dysfunctional personality. She needed to be loved with a love she had never known or experienced before. She needed to know God loved her despite her wrong choices and her searching for love in all the wrong places. She couldn't earn that love. She didn't even know it existed. It had to be God reaching down to an unworthy sinner and giving her an extraordinary gift of love. Her messed up life was only a symptom of her search for meaningful love and fulfillment. She was thirsting for lasting love, unconditional love, a love that would never fade away. Jesus offered her that love of the Father. This is what Paul called the indescribable gift. *"Thanks be to God for his indescribable gift!"* (2 Corinthians 9:15)

Closing Thought
If you are a believer trying to bring others to Jesus, stop trying to correct their lives. Let Jesus give them the indescribable gift of a new life. He will work out the kinks as the Holy Spirit begins to give them new convictions, values and directions. We aren't called to FIX people. Jesus does that. Proclaim Christ and the free gift. Let God do the house cleaning.

Prayer
Lord Jesus, it amazes me that you left your ivory palaces to come to earth to save me! How can you love me so much? Why would you bother? It takes my breath away when I begin to fathom the depths of your love for me. Forgive me Lord for ever thinking that I deserve your love and favor. Your gift of forgiveness and a new life is more than I can ever repay. And on top of that you gave me everlasting life and a home in heaven that is beyond my wildest expectations. Thank You Jesus!

Discuss Together
1. What's the best or most extraordinary gift you ever gave or received? What was the most expensive gift you were ever given? Share your story with your group.
2. What is the most expensive gift you ever gave? To whom? Why?
3. Have you ever really given a gift that "cost you something," not in terms of money but that was a real sacrifice for you to give it? What was it? To whom? Why?

Day 15
My Lamb of God

The next day John saw Jesus coming toward him and said;
*"Look, **the Lamb of God**; who takes away the sin of the world!"*
-- John 1:29

Lambs are cute. At one time in my life my father-in-law was a manager of a sheep ranch. I got to see recently birthed lambs as they struggled to take their first steps. Everyone wanted to hold them. Everyone wanted to cuddle them. They were so cute. When John the Baptist said, *"Behold the Lamb of God"* he wasn't thinking cute – far from it. Seeing a lamb die is sad, but offering your pet first born lamb was hard to let go. But what we don't see here is what every Jewish family had in mind when they heard those words.

The context was that Passover was near. (John 2.12) People all over Palestine were preparing to journey to Jerusalem for the feast of Passover. It was one of the three feasts required by law for all adult males to attend. People were grooming their specially selected lamb for Passover. Many more would buy a lamb of the many flocks being led to Jerusalem. Sheep were being moved in flocks thoughout Palestine toward Jerusalem. What most of us miss here is the pathos, the emotional feelings, that surged through a Jew at Passover. Josephus, the Jewish historian, calculated the numbers of lambs slain at Passover to be 256,500! Each lamb from eight days old to a year old could represent 10-20 people. They would line up before the priests in two rows (24 sets of lines) with golden and silver bowls catching the blood and passing it forward to the altar. It is not possible for our western antiseptic minds to embrace the bloody horror of more than 200,000 lambs being slain!

Imagine standing before a priest with your lamb cradled in your arms as it utters pathetic bleating as it too observed the bloody massacre around it. As the designated family member you would have to hold the lamb while the priest slit its throat and watch as the blood to flow into the provided basins. The lamb would die in your arms. Add to that that this event was repeated by every family every year. Now, see and hear John pointing out Jesus and crying, *"Behold the Lamb of God who takes away the sin of the world."*

Closing Thought

Jesus Christ was God in flesh come to earth with one purpose in mind, to save his people from their sins. That's the point. He came to die, not for himself, but for you and me. He was the Lamb of God, the only spotless lamb that could be a satisfactory offering for sin, once for all. Jesus said, *"And I, if I be lifted up will draw all men unto me."* If you want to lead men to Jesus Christ, don't try arguing evolution or theology. Tell them about how Jesus died as God's Lamb, to take away our sin.

Prayer

Precious Lord Jesus, you died for me. I'm stunned. Why would you do that for me? Why would you die for me? But there was no other way to save me from my sin. So, thank you for offering the ultimate sacrifice and taking my place on the cross. You paid a debt I could never ever pay. You are my Savior. You are my Lamb of God.

Discuss Together

1. Have you ever had to slaughter a lamb? A chicken? A pig? Rabbits? Tell your story. What was that like? How did you feel killing an innocent animal?
2. Most of us aren't shepherds and we've never had a little lamb. But many of us have pets. What is your favorite pet? What if you had to put down your pet to save someone's life? Would you be willing to do it?
3. Jesus was more than God's pet, more than a favorite lamb – he was his one and only Son. He laid down his son's life for you.

Day 16
My Resurrection

I am **the resurrection** and the life. He who believes
in me will live, even though he dies; -- John 11:25

My
Resurrection

John 11:25

"I am the resurrection and the life." I bet you
haven't heard that word bounced around in
everyday conversation. It seems to be a strictly
religious word. Some Jews, most Jews, believed
in a resurrection, a day when all the dead would
be brought back to life. Pharisees believed in it,
Sadducees did not. Jesus took a religious term
and applied it to himself. He wasn't trying to be
religious. He was stating a fact, a truth about
himself.

I like playing with words as a writer and public speaker. Words mean
things. Sometimes a word loses its "pow!" It gets used so often it no
longer makes us sit up and listen. It becomes insipid, overused, and
ineffective. We call that a "banal" or "hackneyed" word. I think
"resurrection" being used only at Easter has become a hackneyed
expression. How can we say "Resurrection" with fresh words? I turn to a
thesaurus that gives synonyms of words. Here are some alternatives to
"resurrect": life-restorer, jump starter, resuscitator, or defibrillator. Take
your pick. I like "breath of life."

Jesus said, *"I am the resurrection and the life (the life-giving breath). I
bring dead things to life. I make dead things live again."* Whether they
have been dead three days, or a century, or even three thousand years it
doesn't matters to Him. He is the Life-giver. He speaks and dead bones
live again. Think about it. Jesus ruined every funeral he ever attended.
Even in His own death the dead were raised. Then to finish off the work
of resurrecting dead things He rose from the dead himself to prove he
has the power of life and death.

Israel was dead, useless, destroyed by enemies and no longer a nation,
but God promised to bring her back from the dead. He did so by taking
Ezekiel to a valley of dry bones, *"The hand of the LORD was upon me,
and he brought me out by the Spirit of the LORD and set me in the
middle of a valley; it was full of bones. He led me back and forth among
them, and I saw a great many bones on the floor of the valley, bones that
were very dry. He asked me, "Son of man, can these bones live?" I
said, "O Sovereign LORD, you alone know." Then he said to me,
"Prophesy to these bones and say to them, `Dry bones, hear the word of
the LORD! This is what the Sovereign LORD says to these bones: I will*

make breath enter you, and you will come to life." (Ezekiel 37:1-5) So
God did it with the Word of His power and by His Spirit.

Closing Thought

**So, what's dead and hopeless in your life situation? He who 'brings
dead things to life' delights to work his Life-Giving power on you. Is
it your marriage? Your spouse? Your children? Your career? Your
body or your brain?   It doesn't matter to him. When he speaks the
word, dead things revive, they live again. Call on him today.**

Prayer

**Lord, I admit there are some things in my life that once were alive
and vibrant, but now they are dying or are already cold and dead. I
need you to revive me and bring my dead heart back to life. Oh,
Resurrection Voice, speak the word and it will live again.**

Discuss Together

1. Just for fun have someone start off the study by singing the old
    negro spiritual "Them Bones Them Bones Them Dry Bones." Can
    you remember the words? Can you connect all the bones properly?
2. Have you ever found a dead body, or uncovered a skeleton? Have
    you found a fossil? Tell us about how and where you found them.
3. Do you have any "dry bones" that need to live again? What was
    once alive and well in your life but is now dead?
4. 'Revival' is when God sends an awakening to a church or individual
    that was dead or dying and He brings it back to life. Have you ever
    seen a dead church get revived? Tell us about it.
5. Do you need to be revived? (something in me has died, something in
    me stinks) What area? Do you have a loved one who needs revival
    that you should pray for?

Day 17
My Life

*""I am the way and the truth and **the life**.*
No one comes to the Father except through me. -- John 14:6

My Life

John 14:6

In the previous study we have already seen that Jesus is the Resurrection. Now let's focus on him being the Life. What did he mean by that? John 1:4 says, *"In him was life, and that life was the light of man."* Again and again we see John spotlighting "The Life" as Jesus. His focus, his attention is on "That Life" as being the most important life that ever lived. That one solitary life makes all the difference for all eternity.

The One-and-Only life is unique in all creation. Just as God, the Father, has life in himself, so he has given the Son to have life in himself. (John 5:26) In conjunction with being the Resurrection (John 11:25) he says he's also the life. *"I am the resurrection and the life."*

The highlight of this dual name (Resurrection and Life) is that he is the Life-Giver. In the old KJV it is (*zoopoieo*) from "*zoon*" from which we get the word zoo, or living creatures. The second part of that word, "*poeio*" means to make, render, produce or author. So, combining them we get the term "Life- Giver." Resurrection is Life-Restorer, and "The Life" is Life-Giver.

He gives "everlasting life." *"He that believes in me though he were dead yet shall he live. And whoever lives and believes in me shall never die."* (John 11:25) It is the contrast of these two titles compared and clarified. "Whoever dies believing – shall live" (v.25a) and "Whoever is alive and believes – never dies." (v. 26)

The only way to get to heaven then is to get life from The Life. That is, to get to heaven you need to be given everlasting life, and that life is in the Son. *"He who has the Son has life, he who does not have the Son, has not life."* I John 5:12

It's simple. He alone has immortality as Paul says to Timothy. He doesn't give out tickets to the Heaven Train. He doesn't give out immortality. He alone is immortal. So, whoever receives the Son has life. He is everlasting life. He is immortal. Eternal life is not some ticket you are awarded or sign up for. Eternal life is in the Son himself. If you've got Jesus in you, you've got everlasting life. You were dead in trespasses and sin, but now you are alive because The Life lives in you. That's what it means to be born again, to pass from death unto life.

Closing Thought
Your only guarantee of heaven is Jesus. If you've got Jesus you've got life! Without him you're dead. Without him you're sentenced to death in hell already. When you have Jesus within your life you are assured of heaven.

Prayer
Forgive me, Lord, for thinking salvation is based on something I do, or a ticket I paid for. I understand now you are my ticket. Without you I can do nothing, and am going nowhere. Come into my heart and life Lord Jesus. Give me everlasting live.

Dig and Discuss:
1. When were you born? Date, day of the week, time? Your parents were given a birth certificate. What does that certificate prove?
2. When were you born again? Date, day of the week, time? Are you sure? How are you sure of your birth?
3. Are you sure you've been born again in Christ? You may not remember the day or the date, but if you have been born again there was a starting point. Think back to your earliest recollection of opening your heart and inviting Jesus Christ into your life. Share that experience. What do you remember about it? Where were you? How did it come about?

Day 18
My Light

*Then Jesus spoke again unto them, saying. I am **the light** of the world: he that follows me shall not walk in darkness, but shall have the light of life: -- John 8:12*

My Light

John 8:12

It is virtually impossible to describe light. How do you describe light to a blind man? How do you explain light to a scientific person? It takes an Einstein mentality to begin to comprehend what light is. But Jack London does a wonderful job describing a baby wolf born in a cave who is drawn by light to illustrate the importance and power of light.

"This was the mouth of the cave and **the source of LIGHT.** He had discovered that it was different from the other walls long before he had any thoughts of his own, any conscious volition. It had been an irresistible attraction before ever his eyes opened and looked upon it. The **LIGHT from it had beaten upon his sealed lids**, and the eyes and the optic nerves had pulsated too little, spark-like flashes, warm- colored and strangely pleasing. The life of his body and of every fiber of his body, the life that was the very substance of his body and that was apart from his own personal life, **had yearned toward this LIGHT** and urged his body toward it in the same way that the cunning chemistry of a plant urges it toward the sun.

Always, in the beginning, before his conscious life dawned, he had crawled toward the mouth of the cave. And in this his brothers and sisters were one with him. Never, in that period, did any of them crawl toward the dark comers of the back-wall. **The LIGHT drew them** as if they were plants; the chemistry of the life that composed them **demanded the LIGHT** as a necessity of being; and their little puppet-bodies crawled blindly and chemically, like the tendrils of a vine. Later on, when each developed individuality and became personally conscious of impulsions and desires, **the attraction of the LIGHT increased.** They were always crawling and sprawling toward it, and being driven back from it by their mother.

It was in this way that the grey cub learned other attributes of his mother than the soft, soothing, tongue. In his **insistent crawling toward the LIGHT**, he discovered in her a nose that with a sharp nudge administered rebuke, and later, a paw, that crushed him down and rolled him over and over with swift, calculating stroke. Thus he learned hurt; and on top of it he learned to avoid hurt, first, by not incurring the risk of it; and second, when he had incurred the risk, by dodging and by

retreating. These were conscious actions, and were the results of his first generalizations upon the world. Before that he had recoiled automatically from hurt, as he had **crawled automatically toward the LIGHT.** *After that he recoiled from hurt because he knew that it was hurt.*
-- White Fang, by Jack London, Part 2, Chapter 3

What a wonderful painted word picture of the importance of light. Life seeks out light just as we seek out oxygen to breathe. Light has a tremendous drawing power. It is built into man to want light and to seek it out at all costs. Jesus is that Light of the World that attracts every man who comes into the world.

Closing Thought
Jesus is the light that shines out to every man in the world. Every man is born with the innate need for light. He is drawn to the light. He craves light. He is driven to pursue the light. Only a blind man can't see the light. But even so, he still needs the LIGHT!

Prayer
Lord, you have drawn me to you in the midst of the dark night of my soul. My darkened heart needed you, yet I hated the light that I so desperately needed. Thank you for your persistence in penetrating my darkness and shining into me the light of your love.

Dig and Discuss
1. Have you ever been trapped in a dark room, a cave, or a tunnel? How did you feel when there was absolutely no light at all? Describe that event as you remember it.
2. Were you afraid? If so, why did it make you fearful?
3. Saint John of the Cross, an ancient man of God wrote about the "dark night of the soul." Have you ever had a period in your life when you felt like you were trapped in a dark night of your soul? What was that like? How did you get out of that dark place?

Day 19
My Lion of Judah

"Weep no more! Look, **the Lion** of the tribe of Judah,
the Root of David, has won the victory. He is worthy..." -- Revelation 5:5

The lion is the symbol of God's victory over all the powers of the enemy. The lion is a powerful and intimidating creature. Proverbs 30:30 says, *"A lion is strongest among beasts, and does not turn away for any enemy."* As such, the lion is a perfect illustration of Jesus Christ. The lion in biblical terms is not a terror to the people of God, but rather to God's enemies.

No lion story is more terrifying than that of the true story of Lt. Col. John Henry Patterson's encounter with two man-eating lions while building a railway bridge over the Tsavo River in Kenya in 1898. During a nine month period two man-eating lions stalked the workers' campsites, dragging Indian workers from their tents at night and devouring them. They were responsible for the deaths of 135 construction workers on the Kenya-Uganda Railway from March through December 1898. It was the inspiration for the movie *"The Ghost and the Darkness"* in 1996. It is a terrible true story of the terror a lion can bring. A lion is a powerful, hungry, and nearly impossible foe that stealthily approaches its prey and springs on it without warning.

Jesus is depicted as the Lion of Judah, a terrible and deadly foe to the enemy that would steal God's children. He is not a terror to those he protects. He is a terror to the one who exists to "steal, kill and destroy." Jesus is on the prowl for the enemy who invades the lives of His children. He will tear the enemy to shreds when we call upon His name.

C.S. Lewis portrays the Lion in a similar light. The Lion Aslan is the hero in the fictitious world of *The Chronicles of Narnia*. He is the king of the lands of Narnia. He is a huge and terrible lion. But he is both ferocious and kind. He is kind to the children of the Kingdom, and mighty devourer to the wicked. When Lucy, one of the children in the story, first hears of the Lion of Narnia, she asks Mr. Beaver, "Is he—quite safe?" Mr Beaver responded, "Safe? Who said anything about safe? 'Course he isn't safe. But he's good. He's the King, I tell you." Jesus is that good Lion in the story of Narnia. He is the good and powerful Lion of Judah in the story of Israel.

Closing Thought

What are you afraid of? Are you afraid the enemy, the devil, that old serpent is going to attack you and eat you for lunch? He will not. He cannot, for the Lion of Judah stands as a ready guard over His children. *"Nothing shall by any means harm you."* You are safe in the palm (paw) of His hand. *"Greater is He that is in you than he that is in the world."* (1 John 4:4)

Prayer

Lord, I am reminded of Scripture that says, *"It is a fearful thing to fall into the hands of the Living God"* and *"Our God is a consuming fire."* Those images sometimes make me afraid of you. I don't want to be afraid of you. A picture of a lion strikes fear into my heart. Teach me to know that you have defeated the only enemy against me, and that as a lion you have won the victory and can frighten off the enemy whenever he is near. Help me to believe that no foe can harm me when you are near.

Discuss Together

1. What animal have you encountered that strikes the most fear into your heart?
2. Have you ever been mauled by a lion, kicked by a horse, bitten by a dog or snake? Tell your experience and your caution now around such an animal.
3. Have you heard any true nightmare stories of people being mauled by a bear, wolf, or other wild animal? Tell that story.

Day 20
My Morning Star

*We have also a more sure word of prophecy; whereunto ye do well that you take heed, as unto a light that shines in a dark place, until the day dawn, and **the morning star** arise in your hearts: -- 2 Peter 1:19*

The word "day star" in Greek, the original language of the New Testament, meant the planet Venus, which is the brightest and first star of the morning announcing a new day. It brought hope for those who were working long night shifts as sailors or shepherds. I used to work as a night watchman on the midnight shift during my college days. I remember how long the nights would be. But then toward dawn a star would outshine them all, and even as the sun began to rise, this star remained in the sky until the sun was fully up. That's Jesus! He is the day star of the Father. He is our hope and assurance of a new day. He is the first light of our eternal day. We keep our eyes fixed on him who brings us hope for a bright tomorrow. That's one reason the star the wise men saw in the east was significant. It heralded a new day and a new beginning.

In golf Mulligans may be used to "do over" any shot. Any drive, fairway shot or putt that didn't work very well or were "muffed" get a chance to be redeemed by doing them over. The term "Mulligan" in golf is a second shot allowed by an opponent and not counted on the score when the first shot was hideously muffed (or missed altogether). Usually it happens on the drive, although not always. Needless to say, ignoring the first stroke happens only in "friendly" golf, not in professional or "serious" golf. Tiger Woods is never given a Mulligan when he plays tournaments.

The do-over was one of childhood's most powerful rites, for it exerted our dominion over the laws of space and time. The clock was rolled back; the game was restored to its exact status as before, before the contested event and play was resumed. If the original play was particularly important and the second attempt was dramatically different (e.g. the player striking out instead of hitting a multi-base shot as in the original play), the do-over might be invoked again. This do-over would give the team another chance, thereby insuring that the second time around might be better than the first.

Closing Thought

Jesus is the Do-Over-King. He makes everything new. He loves doing it. He took the earth when it was without form and void and darkness was everywhere and he turned it into a fertile land. Give him your worthless messes and He will make it over anew.

Prayer

Lord, today I am remembering all my screw ups, all my failures, all my bad decisions. I've made a mess of things. I need a do over. I need a make over. I need a complete overhaul, a rebuild. I give you this heap of junk I've made of my life and ask you to take it and remake it into something beautiful and worthwhile. In Jesus' name, Amen.

Discuss Together

1. Share some terrible screw up you have made sometime in the past. How did it come about? How did you get through it?
2. Do you know someone who really messed up their life through sinful habits or bad decisions? Share their story.
3. Has the Lord rebuilt your ruined places? Share how God has worked to restore your life to Him.

Day 21
My Great Physician

*"It is not the healthy who need **a doctor**, but the sick."* -- Luke 5:31

I find Jesus' healing ministry interesting and even funny at times. He seemed to ask funny questions like: "What do you want me to do? Do you want to get well?" Well, dah! Doesn't everybody want to get well? So, why did he ask such questions? The fact is there are many who want to get over their immediate sickness without thought of healing other more important issues in their lives. Jesus wanted to do more than make people physically well. He wanted to heal body, soul and spirit. He used the reading of Isaiah 61:1-3 to introduce his ministry of healing. It wasn't a superficial healing of making people feel better, but of course, we all want to feel better. The healing he promised was deep down, deeper than a deep tissue massage healing. It was the healing of the heart, the emotions, the sting of sin, and body ailments that keep us from being everything God wants us to be.

The history of medicine is an interesting study. All through time men have known that sickness is a mystery and have addressed the alignment of the stars, the cycle of the moon, the vapors within the body, and a myriad of strange medications to try to solve man's issues with pain and disease.

We think we live in an age of enlightened medicines and treatments, but so did every age from the Greeks to the British medical society. One day we may look back and stand appalled at our own attempts to cure the body. If you don't think so, just listen to the medical advertisements on TV along with the warnings of the dangers of the medicines they are asking you to beg your doctor for.

Here are a few folk medicines that attempt to heal the body. There seem to be a lot of onions, spiders, and stinky things that do a body good.

- Fever – chop up raw onions, put them into a linen cloth, and tie it to the child's feet overnight.
- Headaches – put slices of raw onions on your forehead and securely wrap a cloth soaked in alcohol around your head.
- Nosebleeds – pack a spiderweb into your nose.
- Sore Throat – Take a piece of raw bacon fat and tie a string around it. Hold the string as you swallow the fat and bring it back up. Do this a half dozen times. Then take a black cashmere stocking that has been worn for a week (Eew!), sprinkle the sole with eucalyptus

and place that against your throat. Wrap the rest of the stocking around your neck securely and go to bed.

- Small Pox – Eat a fried mouse.
- Arthritis – Mix turpentine with an egg and animal fat or vegetable oil, and rub it on your skin.
- Bad Dreams – Rub garlic on the soles of your child's feet.
- Bed Wetting – Have the child chew on a cinnamon stick throughout the day, especially before bedtime.
- Bleeding – put a spider web on the cut.

You can see how strange our remedies must be to God. Well, give us credit, we try. Jesus encountered a woman who tried it all and spent all she had on doctors. Then she tried Jesus. She was healed immediately. Take your sickness to Jesus first.

Closing Thought
My Great Physician gives no shots nor causes pain. He doesn't bribe us with Juicy Fruit gum or lollipops. He doesn't need to. His visits are always remedial, comforting and restorative. Oh, and he never turns anyone away! Ever! His office is always open and he is always in. He's touched by the feeling of our infirmities. The only injection Jesus gives is joy and peace. Touch him and he will touch you.

Prayer
Lord, I have to admit that many times in my sickness and pain I am more concerned about my body feeling well, than my spirit being touched by you. There are pains in me that are not physical at all. They are deep emotional hurts and wounds that need an inner touch. Today I bring you the hurt and diseases in me that are not physical, or that just show up as wounds and pain on the outside. Heal my heart. Heal my broken spirit. Heal my depression. Heal my sad heart. Heal my broken relationships. Heal my anger. Heal my bitterness. In Jesus Name, Amen.

Discuss Together
1. What is the worst disease, sickness or injury you ever had?
2. Did you ever have a near death sickness? When was that? What was it? What happened?
3. Have you ever seen anyone healed? Who was it? What was the disease?
4. Have you ever experienced the Lord's miraculous healing? Share your story.

Day 22
My Protector

*Holy Father, **protect** them by the power of your name—the name you gave me--so that they may be one as we are one. -- John 17:11*

Bulldogs

You've probably heard the old expression "As tenacious as a bulldog." Abraham Lincoln used the expression to describe General Grant. A bulldog has the unusual capacity to lock its jaw on its prey and not let go. It has been documented that even after death a bulldog's jaw has to be pried open. This "bulldog" determination to hold us is pictured in Jack London's description of White Fang, the wolf-dog's battle with a bulldog. The bulldog was smaller than White Fang and low to the ground. Once he got a grip on White Fang's throat he refused to let go until White Fang's owner beat the bulldog nearly to death to extricate his champion dog.

Pitbulls

Pitbulls don't have the jaw-locking mechanism that bulldogs have, but they are just as tenacious about letting go. One author describes them this way:

"Each month, the media reports one incident after another of pitbulls attacking other dogs, horses, livestock and people and refusing to let go even after being kicked, beaten, stabbed, tased, pepper sprayed and shot. In October 2009, a pit bull had to be given a lethal injection after it killed one small dog, injured another small dog and then hung on to the owner's hand for 20 minutes. In August 2010, an animal shelter's staff were forced to give a pit bull a lethal injection when they could not stop it from attacking another shelter dog. In Alton, IL a pitbull was shot when it attacked a police officer serving a warrant. Its jaws had to be pried off of the officer's foot AFTER it was killed. In 1991, a pitbull latched on to a little boy and had to be killed to stop the attack and loosen the grip. In May 2012, police fired two rounds into a pitbull during an attack on another dog. The pitbull was not fazed, the police fired another dozen rounds killing it. In Malaysia, a bull terrier bolted from a house and attacked a jogger. A good Samaritan driving by saw the attack and stopped to assist the 74 year old man. He beat the pitbull with an umbrella until it broke and still the animal remained undeterred and kept its jaw locked on the jogger's neck."

Jesus is not a bulldog or a pitbull, but I believe God created such animals to illustrate something about His own character. **He will never let you go! Ever!**

It is quite amazing to me what Jesus said about his power to keep us and protect us. *"And I give unto them eternal life; and they shall never perish, neither shall any man _pluck_ them out of my hand. My Father, which gave them me, is greater than all; and no man is able to _pluck_ them out of my Father's hand."* (John 10:28)

I am surprised (but I suppose I shouldn't be) at how many believers worry that they are beyond Christ's keeping power. So strong is this fear and false guilt that even when they encounter strong biblical truths to the contrary they cry out, "Not so! I can fall away!" Friends, we are not saved in part or half way. We are saved to the uttermost by Him who promised never to let us go, never to leave us or forsake us, and to keep us from falling and present us faultless before His throne. He is able to keep you!

Closing Thought
If you've been raised in an insecure family or church you may have trouble entering the security we have in Christ. God never intended his children to feel insecure or unsafe in his hands. He never intended for us to feel "at risk" anymore than a good parent wants to make their child fearful of their steadfast and never-ending love. He keeps us! We don't keep him. We don't hold him. He holds us! And He will never let us go!

Prayer
Lord, I've felt so long that I had to hang on to you for dear life and that if I failed you in some way I'd lose your love and you'd abandon me. I feel like if I don't live up to your expectations you'd let go of me and I would be lost. Forgive me for thinking your love and grace were that frail. You keep me in the hollow of your hand, so there I will rest in you.

Discuss Together
1. Have you ever felt unloved and or abandoned? Did anyone ever put you out with the trash or leave you abandoned on the street as a child?
2. Why would you ever be tempted to think God would abandon you like that? Where do you think those thoughts come from?
3. Study these security passages, attempt to memorize them and claim Jesus as your keeper.

Day 23
My Rabboni

Jesus said to her, Mary. She turned herself and said to him,
***Rabboni**, which is to say, Master. -- John 20:16*

Mary Magdalene encountered the resurrected Jesus near the tomb. Her eyes were clouded with tears and her mind confused because his body is missing. She perceived a man behind her and thought that it was the gardener. She begged him to tell her where the body was so she could carry it away. Then Jesus said one word that jolted her. He called her by name, *"Mary."* She immediately recognized that voice as the one she loved. Her response was a one-word Aramaic word, a love response, *"Rabboni!"*

Commentators wonder why John records this Hebrew word response instead of just recording the translated word "Master" or "Teacher." There is a reason. This word was an endearing word that could only be conveyed in one's own natural language. It carried with it the meaning "my prince of teachers," or "my precious teacher." Perhaps John knew this was Mary's pet word for Jesus during her life.

Mary Magdalene is an interesting character in the story of Jesus. All four of the Gospels mention her. Luke 8:2 informs us that she was a sinful woman out of whom the Lord cast seven devils. It was she who took an alabaster jar of ointment worth a full year's wages, and pouring it on Jesus' head and feet, then wiping his feet with her hair while weeping. Mary Magdalene was "in love" with Jesus, but not in the romantic sense depicted by some trendy humanistic authors. She was forgiven much, therefore she loved much.

Just about everyone likes a good love story. It's the fodder for most movies and novels written these days. Love is an amazing thing. People in love do crazy things!

Francis Chan, in his book, Crazy Love, has some great things to say about love,

> *"When you are truly in love, you go to great lengths to be with the one you love. You'll drive for hours to be together, even if it's only for a short while. You don't mind staying up late at night to talk. Walking in the rain is romantic, not annoying. You'll willingly spend a small fortune on the one you are crazy about. When you are*

apart from each other, it's painful, even miserable. He or she is all you think about; (You are obsessed) you jump at any chance to be together."

Jesus longs for us to fall in love with him more than all the other loves this earth has to offer. When speaking to the Church at Ephesus in Revelation 2:4 Jesus complimented the church on its good works and solid theology. But he said, *"I have one thing against you. You have lost your first love."* Are you enamored with Jesus as you once were? Do you still cherish that name that is above every name, or has it lost some of its luster? When you say Jesus' name is there still that awe and adoration that the word "Rabboni" held for Mary?

Closing Thought
Are you in love with Jesus, your Lord and Master? This love relationship with Jesus is essential to having a saving faith in him. You can't just like Jesus. You can't just intellectually "accept" him. You must receive him into your heart and life. That's right. You have to invite him to come in and live in you. That's our engagement to Jesus. We are committed to him. We are to be faithful to him. We are to love him with all our heart, mind, soul and strength. That love relationship cannot be mental assent. It must be a real walk of love in daily unbroken communion with him.

Prayer
Dear Jesus, you are more precious than silver to me. You are the lover of my soul. You loved me when I was unloved, unlovely and unlovable. Your love exceeds all other loves. Teach me to know the immensity of that love. Help me to remember it is not I who loved you but you who loved me first and best.

Discuss Together
1. Who was your first love? How old were you? Did it last? If not, why not?
2. Tell us your story of falling in love with your spouse. How did it come about?
3. Have you ever been jilted, dumped, or broken up with? How'd you feel?

Day 24
My Sin Bearer

*Just as Moses lifted up the **snake in the desert**,*
so the Son of Man must be lifted up, that everyone
who believes in him may have eternal life. -- John 3:14-15

Snakes! I hate snakes! Probably the last image of Jesus any of us would want to imagine is a snake, a serpent. It's creepy. It slithers. It writhes along the ground. It's poisonous. It's ugly. And all women and most men are creeped out by the things. So why would God describe his only begotten Son as a serpent? In fact, it is Jesus himself who gives himself this imagery of a bronze serpent.

The serpent plays a diabolical role in Scripture. The book of Revelation calls the enemy, "the great dragon...that old serpent, the devil, and Satan." Almost always the serpent is spoken of in derogatory terms. Almost, but not all.

There are two times when the serpent is used positively. Both appear in Exodus. The first is when Moses and Aaron appeared before Pharaoh. The staff of Moses was thrown down on the ground and became a serpent. The magicians attempted the same and succeeded, but their snakes were eaten up by the rod of Moses.

The second is in Numbers 21:4-9 when the people of Israel were bitten by deadly snakes in the camp and were dying. God instructed Moses to do something otherwise forbidden in the Law. He was to make an image of a bronze serpent and put it on a pole. When the people looked to it in faith, they were healed. They weren't worshipping the snake. They were recognizing that the snake hanging on the pole was their substitute. It was taking the penalty of their sin.

Jesus applies this story to himself. He was that bronze snake lifted up on a pole when he was lifted up on the cross. He took the penalty for sin that we deserved. He became death for us that we might live. He reverses the curse that Satan brought on the earth. It is also interesting that the symbol for a physician is a double snake lifted up on a cross, called a Caduceus. It reminds us of God's promise in Malachi 4:2,

"But for you who revere my name,
the Sun of Righteousness will rise with healing in its wings."

Closing Thought

The power of the cross destroys the work of Satan. Just as looking at the serpent lifted up on the cross saved the sick, so looking to Jesus saves us. And just as calling on the name of the Lord saves us, so calling on His name sends Satan running for cover. Jesus is the victor over all the power of the enemy and nothing shall by any means harm you. He took the venom out of that old serpent, the devil.

Prayer

Lord, I have often found myself cringing in fear of the enemy as I would before a snake. But you have overcome the serpent. You have crushed Satan under your feet. You defeated him at the cross. You are the victor over all the power of the enemy. Therefore, I will keep my eyes on you, not on the enemy, his evil, his attacks or his threats. Greater is he that is in me than he that is in the world.

Discuss Together

1. Have you ever been attacked or bitten by a snake? Share your experience with snakes.
2. How do you feel when you are around a snake? Would you ever permit a snake to crawl around your home? Why not? Can snakes be tamed?
3. Jesus became a curse for us that we might be set free from the curse (Galatians 3:13) Do you have any curses or sins that you have allowed to roam freely in your life or family?
4. Jesus came to set us free from Satan's tyranny. What can you do to declare to Satan that the curse is broken once for all?

Day 25
My Good Shepherd

*I am the **good shepherd**. The good shepherd lays
down his life for the sheep.* -- John 10:11

I'm not a shepherd or even a cattle herder. But, I think I can tell the difference between a good shepherd, a mediocre shepherd and a bad shepherd.

A good shepherd cares about the sheep. He stays with them. He counts them to be sure none are missing. If one is missing, he's on it. He's tenacious, determined, even desperate. He willingly puts himself at risk to go after lost sheep. He calls his sheep by name, not by number. He protects them from predators and poisonous plants. He examines them for wounds and parasites. He pours healing oils on them. When they are weak he picks them up and carries them in his arms. He's willing to lay down his life for his sheep – because they are his.

Mediocre shepherds don't care about the sheep. They are hired hands. It's no loss to them if a sheep wanders away. They don't see themselves as sheep doctors. They think if a sheep stumbles and falls then it ought to dust itself off and get up. If it eats too much or eats the wrong plants and gets sick, well, that's its fault. Maybe they'll learn next time.

Bad shepherds believe in the survival of the fittest. Stuff happens. Sheep get lost and get eaten by predators. A certain percentage of loss is acceptable, even expected. Bad shepherds are about their own safety and comfort. It's a job. It's not worth getting killed over. They believe when the going gets tough, they get going. There are better paying jobs.

Phillip Keller, in his wonderful book *A Shepherd Looks at Psalm 23*, gives us a unique insight into the challenges of a shepherd. I will include an excerpt here concerning a "cast sheep" and what the shepherd must do for her.

A "cast" sheep is a pathetic sight. Lying on its back, its feet in the air, it flails away frantically struggling to stand up, without success. Sometimes it will bleat for help, but generally it lies there lashing about in frightened frustration.

"The way it happens is this. A heavy, fat, or long fleeced sheep will lie down comfortably in some little hollow or depression in the ground. It may roll on its side slightly to stretch out or relax. Suddenly the center of

59

gravity in the body shifts so that it turns on its back far enough that the feet no longer touch the ground...Now it is impossible for it to regain its feet. As it lies there struggling gases begin to build up in the rumen. As these expand they tend to retard and cut off blood circulation to extremities...especially the legs. If it is very hot and sunny a cast sheep can die in a few hours. Buzzards, vultures, dogs, coyotes and cougars all know a cast sheep is easy prey and death is not far off."

Keller continues to explain that a good shepherd keeps count of his sheep and knows immediately when they go missing. He quickly begins his search for the "cast" sheep. As he reaches the sheep he tenderly rolls it over on its side to relieve the gas pressures. Then he gently straddles her and lifts her to her feet while rubbing her limbs to restore circulation to her legs. It may take quite some time but the shepherd gently and patiently talks to her assuring that he will not leave her alone.

Closing Thought
Jesus is the Good Shepherd. He cares. He knows your name. He pursued you when you went astray. He brought you to himself. He healed you by pouring on the oil and wine. He examines you to see that no evil befalls you and no plague comes near your dwelling. He protects you from the evil one, his snares, and his fiery darts. When you are weak he will carry you in his everlasting arms.

Prayer
Lord Jesus, I am so much like a sheep. I overindulge myself in some sin or questionable thought pattern and soon I find myself helplessly toppled over and "downcast" unable to right myself. But thank you for understanding that I am a helpless lamb needing my Shepherd's loving, patient and skilled care. I cannot restore myself, so You restore my soul. Thank you for being my Shepherd.

Discuss
1. Have you ever felt like a "cast sheep"? When? Why? What was it like? Who helped you through that crisis? Share your weaknesses – it's a command in Scripture, *"Confess your faults one to another and pray one for another that you may be healed. And if you have committed any sins they will be forgiven you."* (James 5:15-16)
2. Have you ever bothered to help a "cast sheep" in your circle of friends? Maybe it's a brother fallen into a pit of depression, an addiction to pornography, a romantic infatuation, drug or alcohol dependency, a sinful attitude or habit. James says, *"Whoever turns a sinner from the error of his way will save him from death and cover over a multitude of sins."* (James 5:20)

Day 26
My Absolute Truth

*I am the way and **the truth** and the life.*
No one comes to the Father except through me. -- John 14:6

There's a lot of lying going on in politics these days. I suppose that's always been the case. Someone has said, "How do you know a politician is lying?" The answer: "If his lips are moving." Perhaps that is what Pilate had in mind when he was interrogating Jesus when he said, "What is truth?"

In our day of Facebook and the Internet one has to examine carefully what is true and what is false. Truth is what is absolute, unchanging, permanent, unfaltering, non-eroding and eternal. It's real. It's not a theory. It's not speculation. It's not a guess. It's not one man's opinion. It is what it is. It's what is certain when all else is suspect. It's the guarantee. I saw a post on Facebook the other day showing a picture of Abraham Lincoln and a quote, *"If it is on the Internet then it must be true and you can't question it." – Abraham Lincoln*

Science is not truth. It's always evolving, correcting and changing its beliefs. Theology is not truth. It's man's attempt to articulate truth, but it too follows fads and the winds of opinion and consensus. Truth is not relative. There's no "What's true for me may not be true for you." Truth is not flexible. It doesn't ebb and flow. It doesn't go with the flow of human whims.

If a judge puts you on a witness stand he will ask you to raise your right hand and place your left hand on the Bible and then he will ask you, "Do you swear to tell the truth, the whole truth, and nothing but the truth so help you God?" The assumption is that you will say, "yes." But that doesn't guarantee you will tell the truth.

Jesus was, is and always will be Truth and truthful. He is God and God cannot lie. (Hebrews 6:18, Titus 1:2) He doesn't make wild assertions or crazy exaggerations. He doesn't make things up. He doesn't play fast and loose with the truth. What he says is always absolutely and eternally true.

Truth is absolute. Truth is what God says. *"Let God be true and every man a liar."* (Romans 3:4) So when Jesus said, *"I am the Truth"* he wasn't just saying he tells the truth. He was saying, "I am the absolute truth. There IS no other truth. There is no other absolute." Just as his word is true, *" Not the smallest letter, not the least stroke of a pen, will by any means disappear from the Law until everything is accomplished, heaven and earth shall pass away but my words shall never pass away."* (Matthew 5:18) He is Truth. He was saying "My character and words are absolute, they do not change. You will find truth nowhere but in me."

Closing Thought
It is a good idea to not call God a liar. Many believers harbor resentment in their hearts that somehow God lied since they didn't get what they prayed for. Friend, God does not lie. Ever! His promises are always true. Look for the blame somewhere else.

Prayer
Lord, I have to admit that sometimes I have a feeling that you lied and your promises are not true. But you have affirmed over and over that you are faithful and true. Help me then to lean on your promises for my life. "Keep me and protect me in your truth. Your word is truth."

Discuss Together
1. Have your ever told a lie? Have you ever been caught in a lie? Think of an instance and share it with others.
2. Do you know anyone who is a chronic liar? Is there someone you don't trust because too often they have lied or deceived you?
3. Have you ever had someone break a promise, or have you broken a promise?

Day 27
My Only Way

*I am **the way** and the truth and the life.*
No one comes to the Father except through me. -- John 14:6

"*The Way*" is mentioned three times in three verses. Jesus was baiting his disciples with the questions about the way.
Verse 4 "...you know THE WAY to the place I am going..."
Verse 5 "How can we know THE WAY...?"
Verse 6 "I am THE WAY..."

The whole conversation is a set-up to present this one truth, "*I am the way.*" In the Greek, the language of the New Testament, "*hodos*" or "way" means 'highway, journey, road or path'. The word "*hodos*" (3598) is used 99 times in the New Testament, most often referring to highways, and sometimes about "the way" to God."

In Jesus' day the Romans had built superhighways, some of which are still in existence today. They are called "vias" or thoroughfares. They were broad, paved with cobblestones and made travel throughout the Roman Empire fast and easy. We still use the expression "all roads lead to Rome" today because it was true. Every Roman road eventually ended up in the city of Rome. However, Jesus was highlighting the difference: all ways, roads, paths don't lead to God. Only one does. That one road is Jesus.

Have you ever been lost? Most of us think we have a pretty good sense of direction. But there are times when all of us become disoriented and lose our way. Daniel Boone was once asked if he every got lost in the deep forests of early America. He responded, "No, I've never been lost, but I have been bewildered for three days."

There are lots of stories of good people losing their way. There is an incident in the story of Captain Kidd in which Commodore Thomas Warren (nickname, Wrong-Way Warren), commander of a squadron of a hundred ships, loses his way and repeatedly miscalculates his position. He was unable to find Madeiras which is situated 200 miles off the coast of Africa. He lost more than half of his crew through starvation, dehydration, and disease while he guessed his way around the Atlantic.

There's the famous story of Douglas Corrigan (Wrong-Way Corrigan) who set off in an airplane from New York to California but landed in Ireland by mistake. He claimed it was a navigational error caused by heavy cloud cover that hid important landmarks and low light conditions causing him to misread his compass. (So he claimed.)

The Scripture reminds us that *"all we like sheep have gone astray."* (Isaiah 53:6) Proverbs tells us *"There is a way that appears right unto man, but in the end it leads to death."* (Proverbs 16:25) Job rightly testified, *"He knows the way that I take, and when I am tried I will come forth as gold."* (Job 23:10)

Jesus tells us that He alone is the Way, the Truth and the Life, and that no one can come to the Father except through Him. He is the Way. He doesn't just show the way or point out the way. Follow Jesus. There's no other way!

Closing Thought
Have you lost your way in this life? Have you been going the wrong direction and thinking all along that you are right? We are not homing pigeons with a natural GPS built into our character. Our compass has been spoiled. The right way is always the Jesus Way. He is the only way out of earthly trouble. He is the only way to the Father. The only way to heaven is to follow him. He knows that way through your wilderness. All you have to do is follow.

Prayer
Jesus, thank you for providing a way for me to enter heaven. Thank you that you do not just point me the way I should go, you are the WAY. All I need to do is stay close to you and follow in your footsteps and I will not be lost. Help me stay close to you. Better yet, hold my hand and keep me in the Way.

Discuss Together:
1. Have you ever been lost? I mean really lost? Share your story.
2. Talk about the worst roads you have ever traveled.
3. Show the You Tube Video called "Crazy Drive" that depicts traveling by bus on a narrow cliff edge through the mountains.
4. Research or Google Roman Highways, or Vias. What did you find interesting?

Day 28
My Sheltering Wing

*O Jerusalem, Jerusalem…how often would I have gathered
your children together, even as a hen gathers her chicks
under her wings, and you would not! -- Matthew 23:37*

We don't often think of God in the female gender, but then we must remember that God is spirit, and neither male nor female. All illustrations of God are metaphors or anthropomorphisms. God is not a bird and Jesus is not a hen, but the metaphor of wings seems to be great with God. Perhaps he placed birds into His creation for the very purpose of demonstrating His overshadowing wings of protection and his powerful ability to carry us on His wings when we cannot stand on our own.

In several passages God depicts himself as a "hen," but more specifically He describes his sheltering wing. In this passage, as in Matthew 23:37 and Luke 13:34 Jesus likens himself to a mother hen or a nesting, brooding, mother bird. We westerners always think of a chicken, but the word is generic enough to refer to a mother eagle, a mother pheasant, or a mother bluebird. The picture is of the mother hen with wide, safe wings outstretched for her young to run to for protection and shelter in the time of storm or trouble.

There is a wonderful painting of a tempest on a rocky cliff-lined shore. The artist portrays the violence of the wind, the waves crashing, the dark storm clouds, driving rain, and the lightning. Everything in the picture is foreboding except for one small detail. In a small cleft in the rock face is a mother bird, face to the wind, with its wings extended over its chicks in the nest. They are safe and secure under her wings.

Despite many years of flying in aircraft around the world I am still amazed each time that heavy metal contraption powers down the runway and suddenly lifts off into the air carrying 300 passengers and baggage. I always marvel to the Lord, "How is it possible that this heavy machine is able to overcome gravity and soar through the air five miles above the earth?" The answer of course is in physics. The wings create the lift as air moves under and over those extended arms. We are held up and lifted above the power of gravity and death defying turbulence by magnificent wings.

Closing Thought

The message should be clear, He is waiting with outstretched wings in the times of our storms, but we must be willing to run there and take our refuge underneath His wings. The Lord your God wants to carry you on eagles' wings (Exodus 19:4) and to shield you under his wings for eternal protection. Take him today as your wing of protection and deliverance.

Prayer

Lord, I am too earth-bound. I often forget that you are not. You never intended us to live our lives by earthly laws of physics or to pull ourselves up by our own bootstraps. Help me to remember in times of turbulence that you have promised to carry me on the "wings of eagles" when I cannot possibly walk on my own or overcome the obstacles that are too big for my finite strength. Thank you for your everlasting arms!

Discuss Together

1. What is your earliest memory of your mother? What was she doing?
2. As a parent have you ever had to hold your sick baby during the night? How did you feel? Were you willing even to give your life that he/she might live?
3. What circumstances might motivate you to choose this name of the Lord to walk with you through the coming year?

Day 29
My Sanctifier

__Sanctify__ them by the truth; your word is truth.
For them I __sanctify__ myself, that they too may be truly __sanctified__.
-- John 17:17-19

The word "Sanctify" is a strong word. I bet you haven't used it in conversation in a long, long time, if ever. We normal people don't talk this way. This is religious speech. Therefore, to most of us it is irrelevant. It's meaningless.

But Jesus was a practical guy. He spoke the common language of the day known as "*koine*" Greek. He related to common people. Crowds loved to hear him speak. He didn't speak like religious leaders. So, why now does he come up with this specialized religious word? "Sanctify" is to set apart something common, to clean it up and make it a special tool for God's use.

For years we used to camp out as a family. We accumulated a lot of camping equipment that was useful for that rustic experience. One week a missionary friend and I camped out behind our newly built wooden chapel to stand guard against people stealing our construction equipment tools. After we had set up our tent and cooking supplies we suddenly realized we had no bathroom, not even an outhouse. In desperation we looked at our cooking supplies and decided that one particular pot would serve us for that purpose. It worked well. But, you know, I could boil, wash, scrub and scour that pot a hundred times but I could never again use it as a cooking pot. It might be clean and germ free, but I'd always be reminded of its former use.

Only God can take filthy pots and make them sanctified and ready for the Master's use. We must recognize that we are all filthy pots. God's word makes it clear that "*there is none righteous, no not one.*" (Romans 3:10) "*All have sinned and come short of the glory of God.*" (Romans 3:23). And "*if we keep the whole Law and yet offend in one point we are just as guilty of all*" *just* as if we broke every command. (James 2:10) We cannot by our own efforts clean ourselves up for "*the heart is deceitful above all things and desperately wicked.*" (Jeremiah 17:9) For those of us who think we are pretty good we need to understand that God says, "*We are all as an unclean thing, even our righteousnesses are as filthy rags.*" (Isaiah 64:6)

Closing Thought

We are unholy people. We have all failed and come short of glorifying God. So, Jesus took on the task of being sin for us that God might apply to us the righteousness of Jesus to our overdrawn account. But God's not done. He wants to sanctify us wholly, body, soul, and spirit to make us fit vessels for his work. He does this through his word. He washes us daily in the word that we might remain clean. So, let the word of Christ wash over you daily by reading it, meditating on it, and obeying it.

Prayer

Lord, I don't feel very holy. In fact, much of the time I'm conscious of my shortcomings and failures. I need you to make me holy from the inside out. Help me to remember to expose myself every day to your word so that you can cleanse me and make me a fit vessel for your use.

Discuss Together

1. What's the dirtiest most disgusting thing you've ever had to deal with? Diapers, vomit, a fat trap, a dead animal?
2. Who do you think is the worst sinner you have ever met? Don't name names, but think of someone who is so far from God that it's hard to imagine they would ever be saved.

Day 30
My Finisher

*Let us fix our eyes on Jesus, the author
and **finisher** of our faith.* -- Hebrews 12:2

This "Finisher" is an interesting word and concept, that what God begins to do he is able to carry out to completion. Jesus said, as he was dying on the cross, *"It is finished!"* (John 19:30) That is significant! What was finished? The work he came to do was finished as the Lamb of God was sacrificed for the sins of the people. The work of salvation was complete. Now he can save his people from their sins.

Everywhere we look it seems there are unfinished building projects that for one reason or another are never completed.

Most of us have heard of Westminster Abbey in London, England. It is one of the most beautiful churches in the world. But most people don't realize it is not the mother church of England. That honor belongs to Westminster Cathedral just down the street. That cathedral has been under construction since 1885 and has never been finished. Its interior is nothing but unfinished brickwork. Evidently it was too expensive to complete.

One of the most expensive unfinished projects is the Marble Hill Nuclear Power Plant in Indiana. The plant construction started in 1977 and apparently was nearly complete. In 1984 the company abandoned the project after sinking $2.5 billion dollars into getting the reactors to the halfway point. The owners were able to recoup a few million dollars by selling some of the equipment. The plant has been sitting idle for 34 years and is just now scheduled to be demolished.

Evidently this has always been the case since ancient times as well. Jesus was a carpenter and knew all about well-intentioned projects that later were abandoned. He warned about starting projects you cannot afford to finish. (Luke 14:28-30) *"Suppose one of you wants to build a tower. Will he not first sit down and estimate the cost to see if he has enough money to complete it? For if he lays the foundation and is not able to finish it, everyone who sees it will ridicule him, saying, `This fellow began to build and was not able to finish.'"* In contrast Jesus said in John 4:34 *"My food is to do the will of him who sent me and to <u>finish his work</u>."*

Jesus is a "Finish Carpenter." He doesn't do things halfway. The work that he began in you he will keep at until the day you die. It's his promise. IT IS FINISHED!

Closing Thought
When Jesus died on the cross he said, "It is finished" because it was! He completed the work he came to do. Now, the saving us from sin is complete. It's guaranteed! But he's not done with you yet. He is fully able to complete the work he began in you.

Prayer
Lord, you've got a lot of work to do in me and on me. I'm yours, so take me, make me, and remold me into what you long for me to be. Please don't give up on me. I invite you to complete your work you began in me.

Discuss Together
1. Did you ever get an "Incomplete" in a school assignment? How did that make you feel? Do you remember the occasion? What was your excuse for not getting it done?
2. Have you ever started a project and left it unfinished? Your intention was good but your follow through was lacking.
3. What projects are yet unfinished in your life? Perhaps it's a painting, a house project, a building, a hot rod, etc. What would it take to get it finished?

Day 31
My True Vine

*I am **the vine**; you are the branches. If a man remains in me and I in him, he will bear much fruit; apart from me you can do nothing.*
-- John 15:5

Did you ever see a space walk? It's fascinating. There they are, 200 miles above the earth, with no gravity and no air, traveling at 17,500 miles per hour orbiting around earth every 1 ½ hours. The hatch opens and out steps an astronaut with only a small umbilical cord for his life support. He is entirely dependent on that tether. That's the "vine and the branches."

I'm not a farmer or horticulturalist so I don't know much about plants, much less grape vines. There is a wonderful movie titled *A Walk in the Clouds* that effectively mentors us in the cultivation of grapevines as it weaves a romantic tale of love. In the story the vineyard owner in a drunken fit accidentally ignites a fire that rapidly escalates and consumes hundreds of acres of grape vines. All seems a total loss until the hero of the story remembers there is an ancient vine that is the mother of all the vines in the vineyard. It too was burned, but only on the outside. There was still life in the vine to birth new life for a new vineyard to grow.

Jesus was in a large upper room for the Passover meal. It wasn't grape season but there might have been a grape arbor outside one of the windows. Jesus didn't usually teach by grabbing illustrations out of thin air. Generally, he used things at hand as visual aids. I picture Jesus sitting on a window sill as he talked to his disciples in a hot upper room. He spies the grape vine growing near the window and he uses it as an illustration. Or perhaps someone had cut grape vines to decorate the table in the upper room. That would have afforded a great example of a dying branch, one cut off from the vine.

But looking carefully at John's narrative he says just before this verse, *"Come, let us leave."* So this part of the talk might have been on the way to the Mount of Olives. The visual illustration helps. Perhaps they were walking through a recently pruned vineyard. In any event, it was a poignant visual. A grape vine had a hefty trunk Jesus called "the true vine." It was the part of the plant that was anchored into the ground by a healthy root system. Jesus points out the already pruned vine with only a few branches left. Others were scattered on the ground, withered.

He shows the disciples the importance of a branch staying connected to the vine. Without the vine the branches were useless except to be gathered and burned. Jesus is speaking about the importance of an intimate relationship with him, just as he had with the Father. That's the only way they could ever be fruitful and happy.

Closing Thought
The vine and branches metaphor is rich and helpful. Without a close intimate walk with the Savior (abiding) we can do nothing – no fruit, no answered prayers, no love relationship and no joy. Stay close. Stay connected. Stay hungry, my friend.

Prayer
Lord, the impact of this truth is profound on my heart. Without you I can do nothing! Help me live near your heart in absolute dependence on you.

Discuss Together
1. Have you ever visited a vineyard? Where did you go? Did you do some wine tasting? Was it good? Tell us about what you saw and learned.
2. Have you ever smelled ripe grapes on the vine? Describe the smell for others to enjoy. Why were grapes and vineyards so important and frequently mentioned in Scripture?

Day 32
My Righteous Judge

*Moreover, the Father judges no one, but has entrusted all judgment to the Son. And he has given him authority to **judge** because he is the Son of Man…and has given him authority to **execute judgment**, because he is the Son of man.* -- John 5:22, 27

I get terrified when I see the flashing lights of a police car behind me warning me to pull over. Each time, I experience a hot flash of terror, and my blood pressure sky rockets. It doesn't matter if I was speeding or going under the limit, I still feel guilty. So do you! We are intimidated by the authority of a judge!

Judges with gavels and police officers' flashing lights make me feel nervous because I already feel guilty even before being accused of anything. Most of us, if we are honest, carry a certain amount of free-floating guilt that makes us feel guilty even before being accused of a crime or infraction.

So, when I read that Jesus is my Judge it scares me. Perhaps a part of that guilt comes from shouting preachers who wanted to be like Jonathon Edwards in his immortal sermon, "Sinners in the Hands of an Angry God."

It's hard for us who grew up in guilt-based Christianity to feel safe around a judge. When we think of standing before the Judgment Seat of Christ we see ourselves drowning in a pool of guilt.

But think for a moment of the judgment seat of Jesus Christ. It is not a trial unto condemnation because believers have been promised to *"come not into condemnation."* Our judgment is already passed when God sees the blood; He will pass over you. This judgment seat is the award ceremony to receive rewards for things done in this life. It is our graduation ceremony, not our trial.

The Father has committed all judgment to the Son. (John 5:22) His judgment is just. It's not to condemn, but to declare us innocent, to release us, to exonerate us, to declare us NOT GUILTY! Jesus is not, nor ever will be, your prosecuting attorney. He is your advocate to plead the blood that cleanses you from every stain.

Here's the proof. *"Whoever hears my words and believes on him who sent me HAS everlasting life, and WILL NOT BE CONDEMNED, but has passed from death to Life"* (John 5:24)

Closing Thought

A false sense of guilt and condemnation often accompanies the believer because the Spirit of God has made you sensitive to your own failures and sins. Satan is the accuser of the brethren, not God. Jesus does not accuse of sin, he convicts of sin. There is a huge difference. *"If we confess our sins He is faithful and just to forgive us our sins and cleanse us from all unrighteousness."* (1 John 1:9)

Prayer

Lord, help my guilt-ridden soul to no longer fear being cut off by you. You sent Jesus to die for my sins that I might be delivered from condemnation and be forever safe in the arms of Jesus. Forgive my insecure heart for thinking that you are my accuser. You are my Righteous Judge whose righteous laws were fulfilled by Jesus Christ for me. Thank you that there is now NO CONDEMNATION for me.

Discuss Together

1. Did you ever get in trouble in school and have to go to the principal's office or be put in a corner? Or maybe you were raised when corporal punishment was allowed in school. Did you get spanked with a ruler? Did you get swats?
2. Have you ever been pulled over by a policeman? Were you speeding? Why did he pull you over? Were you guilty?
3. Have you ever had to go before a judge and plead your case? Tell us about it. What happened? How did it turn out? Was the judge lenient, merciful, or tough?

Day 33
The Final Absolute Word

*In the beginning was the **Word**, and the
Word was with God, and the **Word** was God.* -- John 1:1

The Word – Rhema, Logos

There are two distinctive words in Greek to say the same thing, "the Word." One was the Greek word LOGOS the other was the Greek word RHEMA.

Most of us have difficulty understanding John's use of the term 'Word" in this passage. That's because the Greek word he used, Logos, is difficult to translate for the modern western reader. "Logos" was a Greek philosophical term that was familiar to his audience. Today most of us aren't Greek nor are we familiar with Greek philosophies. So we are at a loss to understand this word.

The Final Word

John 1:1

The Logos, the Noun

Ancient Greek philosophers (Heraclitus, Parmenides, Aristotle, and Philo (25-50 BC) coined the term *Logos* as they were trying to figure out the origin and meaning of life. Their writings and thoughts on *Logos* are interesting, but we will restrict our comments to Philo, who was a Jew living in a Greek world, called a Hellenistic Jew. He was a Jew and lived closest to the time of Jesus therefore he probably had a great influence on John. He theorized that God was so wholly other that he had to "translate" himself into the material world via his "*Logos*," the part of him that is visible and understandable in the material world. The *Logos* acted on God's behalf in the physical world. Thus he postulated that *Logos* was God's instrument (God's hand) in creation. He wrote, "The Logos of the Living God is the bond of everything, holding all things together and binding all the parts, and preventing them from being dissolved and separated." Does that sound familiar? Read Paul's description of Jesus.

"He is the image of the invisible God, the firstborn over all creation. For by him all things were created: things in heaven and on earth, visible and invisible, whether thrones or powers or rulers or authorities; all things were created by him and for him. He is before all things, and in him all things hold together." - Colossians 1: 15-17

The Rhema

Rhema is the spoken word, whether verbalized audibly or written. *Rhema* means the word or words with which we communicate. *Rhema* is almost always related to how the Spirit of God uses the Word to open our understanding. It is the Word made alive in our hearts as we read it.

It is God opening eyes blinded by Satan so that the truth of the Gospel can shine into us. *Rhema* is that "Ah-ha" moment when God speaks to our hearts.

The Verb
While serving as a missionary in Brazil we were astounded to hear the Brazilian Portuguese translation of this passage that read. *"No princípio era o Verbo, e o Verbo estava com Deus, e o Verbo era Deus."* The literal translation of this is *"In the beginning was the Verb and the Verb was with God and the Verb was God."* They translated this Greek word "Logos" as "Verb." Just as in English a "verb" is a part of speech that expresses action, being, or state of being.

Closing Thought
Jesus is the First and Final Word of God. He encapsulates all the heart and message of the Father to a fallen world. He is the Truth, the final authority. His *"Word is living, active and more powerful than any two-edged sword. It pierces, it penetrates even to dividing soul and spirit, joints and marrow; it judges the thoughts and attitudes of the heart."* (Hebrews 4:12)

Prayer
Lord, I stand in awe of you. How amazing you are! That you created me through Christ makes me feel special. You spoke the word and brought all things into existence. You have all power in heaven and earth. Then you keep all things in your control. You spoke that same Creator Word to my heart and made it come to life. Your words are Spirit and they are life to me. Thank you Jesus.

Discuss Together
1. Most evangelical believers have difficulty understanding the deity of Jesus Christ, that he was and is God. Can you give three clear verses that declare Jesus is God?
2. If you had a conversation with a Mormon or Jehovah's Witness about the deity of Christ, what would you say?
3. What Scripture would you use? What illustrations would you use?

.Day 34
My Provider

*My God will **supply** all your needs according*
to his glorious riches in Christ Jesus. -- Philippians 4:19

One of the great names of the Lord in both the Old and New Testaments is *"My Provider."* In the Old Testament it is *Jehovah-Jireh, the Lord who sees ahead and provides.* (Genesis 22:14) In the New Testament it is Jesus beside me sharing in my every experience, whether in a storm in a wind swept boat, a wedding feast that runs out of wine, a tax debt that comes without notice, or any myriad of daily crises of supply and demand. Know this: it never catches Him by surprise! The Lord knows it before it happens. He has a plan. He doesn't get ruffled, upset, worried, fearful or grumpy. Every crisis is for a purpose and that purpose is for His glory and your good.

My mother was a godly prayer warrior who took everything to God in prayer, but her faith was often tested to the limit. Her example taught us to call on the Lord in every crisis and expect that God will answer in unusual ways.

The most remarkable experience of my childhood was the day God provided bread from an empty cupboard. Dad was on strike or laid off again and food was in short supply. On this ominous day we didn't have any bread in the house. There was nothing. Mom sat us down and told us again the story of George Mueller and how he prayed for food for his orphanage and God always provided. So, that morning she prayed. Then we waited fully expecting that someone would knock on our door with food for the day. No one came. She prayed again and we waited. We had already watched Mom look through all the cupboards as we did in search of something to eat. There was nothing. Old Mother Hubbard went to the cupboard, but this time it wasn't the dog without a bone, it was the kids who were going to go hungry. Again we prayed and waited. Finally Mom got up one more time and searched again for something to feed her children. This time to all of our amazement there was a loaf of bread tucked in a corner that had not been there before. I wish I could go back for a video replay of that scene because I wonder if it was "Wonder Bread." It certainly was manna from heaven.

I'll never forget that miracle. It was God's miraculous intervention in our lives. It served to teach us that the Lord is not uncaring, ignorant of our crisis, or too busy to intervene. God did not say, "God helps those who help themselves." – Ben Franklin did. God helps those who trust Him and cry out to him in their need believing he cares and answers.

Closing Thought

What is your crisis today? What is your great need that you cannot supply? God wants to hear it. He wants you to tell Him all about it. He loves for His children to come to Him for their needs. He permits the crisis so that He can do a miracle. Every miracle came as a result of a problem that man could not solve. So, stop complaining about the crisis and start calling on Jesus. His pockets are deep enough to supply your every need.

Prayer

Lord, I'm a worry wart. I sometimes fear that you aren't aware of my desperate need, or that I'm not important enough for you to care. I don't like to bother you because I often know that I'm not worthy of your rewards. But your love is not for sale to the best behaved or the most lovely child. You love me regardless and promised to never leave me or forsake me. So, Lord be with me in this crisis. Hear my cry and answer me that you might receive all the glory.

Discuss Together

1. Did you ever have a crisis of need? I don't mean a want or just a shortage of something, but a real need, like no food whatsoever.
2. Did you ever have a bill due and no money to pay it? What did you do? Did God answer your prayer? How did He supply?
3. Have you seen God answer the supply need for someone else? Tell us that story?

Day 35
My Potter

*Does not **the potter** have the right to make out of the same lump of clay some pottery for noble purposes and some for common use?*
-- Romans 9:21

God loves to use everyday things to illustrate His character and purposes. Paul is referring to an Old Testament illustration the Lord gave to Jeremiah in chapter 18.

> *This is the word that came to Jeremiah from the LORD: "Go down to the potter's house, and there I will give you my message." So I went down to the potter's house, and I saw him working at the wheel. But the pot he was shaping from the clay was marred in his hands; so the potter formed it into another pot, shaping it as seemed best to him. Then the word of the LORD came to me: "O house of Israel, can I not do with you as this potter does?" declares the LORD. "Like clay in the hand of the potter, so are you in my hand, O house of Israel."*

Imagine Jeremiah leaning on his staff, standing back and watching the master craftsman working clay on his spinning wheel. He starts with a lump of clay. It has nothing notable or special about it. It's just a lump of dirt. Then the master puts just the right amount of clay on the wheel to make what he has in mind. The wheel spins and the master's hands go to work on that worthless piece of clay. Gradually with the right pressure, his fingers adeptly mold the clay into the shape that he had in mind. It might be a cup, a plate, a large water jar, or a tiny vase. Only the master potter knows what he has in mind. He knows how to shape the clay, whether it's too dry, too wet, lumpy or flaky. He is skilled enough that whatever the problem with the clay he is up to the challenge. No clay is too difficult for him. He is the master potter. He knows how to make it into something of great value and usefulness.

That's what Jesus does to us. He is working on the inside to make us what he wants us to be. We are just lumps of clay, just dirt, and nothing special until the Master Potter gets His hands on us. We might be dull, flaky, lumpy, too hard, or too soft but the Master isn't stumped by our imperfections. He can do anything with any lump of clay. He is the Potter and we are the clay.

Closing Thought

Later, to the Corinthians (a lot of dysfunctional Christians) he says, *"But we have this treasure in jars of clay to show that this all-surpassing power is from God and not from us."* (2 Corinthians 4:7) What a wonderful concept! It's not about us. It's about Him! He wants to show the excellency of His power in us. The worse the clay He starts with, the greater His glory in shaping it into a useful vessel.

Prayer

Lord, I get frustrated with myself. I'm not all I want to be for you. I fail. I mess up. I am stubborn. I'm self-centered. But Lord, I'm just a lump of dust you took out of the ground. I'm created from dirt. So, take this lump of clay that I am and make something good out of my life. In Jesus' name, Amen.

Discuss Together

1. Many people either have high self esteem or low self esteem. They either are confident of their worth, or they feel inferior and less than worthy. Which are you?
2. If you feel worthless or unworthy where do you think you developed that idea?
3. Have you ever failed at something? I mean really failed? Maybe it was your marriage, a job, a task you were given? What was it? Tell us about your failure.
4. Aren't you glad God is still working on you? He doesn't give up on you because you fail. He knows you are weak. He knows you fail. That's why He wants to be your Potter.
5. Can you think of other verses that assure us that God is still working on us?

Day 36
My Ransom

*Who gave himself a **ransom** for all, to be testified in due time.*
-- 1 Timothy 2:6

The other day I read about some of the most expensive ransoms ever paid. The common denominator in all these kidnappings was that the victims were children or employees of the very wealthy. No one is going to pay a ransom for a worthless individual. The ransom demanded and paid is equal to the value of the one captured.

One of the most infamous crimes of all time took place in Mach 1932 when Charles Augustus Lindbergh Jr., the 20-month-old son of the renowned aviator, was kidnapped for ransom. Around 8:00 p.m. on March 1 the nurse put little Charles in his crib wrapped in a blanket and fastened with two pins to keep him snug for the night. At 10:00 p.m. she returned to the room to find the baby missing and a note on the windowsill. The note read:

> *Dear Sir!*
> *Have $50,000 ready, $25,000 in $20 dollar bills, $15,000*
> *in $10 bills, and $10,000 in $5.00 bills. In 2-4 days we*
> *will inform you where to deliver the money.*

Unfortunately the ransom was paid, but the infant wasn't returned, and his body was found near the Lindbergh home two months later. Eventually the ransom bills were tracked down and a suspect arrested, tried, and executed. Even though a suspect was captured and executed, the case remains surrounded in controversy to this day. The case remains one of the most mysterious and tragic kidnappings and ransoms ever perpetrated.

One of the most expensive ransoms ever paid was for King Richard the Lionheart. He was ransomed for 150,000 marks in 1190, the estimated equivalent of $3.3 billion today. King Richard was sailing back from the Crusades when bad weather forced him to land in unfriendly territory on the Island of Corfu, in Greece on the Mediterranean Sea. Richard and his men disguised themselves as Knights Templar and made their way back to Europe. But while passing through Vienna he was identified and captured by the unfriendly Leopold V, Duke of Austria. The Duke demanded a ransom of 150,000 marks, two or three times the annual revenue of England. A year later the ransom was paid.

In the case of our ransom, we are apparently poor and worthless sinners, who have no value to be ransomed. But God in his immense love and compassion sent His one and only Son, Jesus Christ, as the ransom payment to deliver us from the hands of the enemy, Satan, who would drag us to hell with him. God's payment of such an awesome price for such wretched sinners will for all time be the greatest ransom every paid!

Closing Thought
The ransom paid by Jesus ends well. Though He gave His life to save us and it seemed that all was lost, Jesus triumphed over death and hell and rose from the dead to prove He was God, and was able to save us to the uttermost capturing the enemy in the process. Here is an awesome thought: You were named on Satan's ransom note, but Jesus paid the price for you to rescue you from eternal death.

Prayer
Oh, Lord, what extreme love you have shown to me, that you would lay down your life to rescue me from certain death and Hell! Thank you, Jesus, my Eternal Ransom.

Discuss Together
1. Ransoms are not common things but occasionally we hear about one in the news. Can you remember any ransom stories from recent news stories? Tell us what you remember about that ransom.
2. If your son or daughter were kidnapped and held for ransom would you pay the ransom asked for? What if it were more than you could come up with, what would you do?
3. How much do you think you would be worth to your wife or husband if you were kidnapped and held for ransom? Would you want to be ransomed?

Day 37
My Great "I Am"

"I tell you the truth," Jesus answered,
*"before Abraham was born, **I am**!" -- John 8:58*

In Exodus chapter three God chose to reveal himself to Moses in the burning bush, not as Elohim, or even YWHY (Jehovah), but as *"I AM."* It is a strange title, but an appropriate descriptor for the God of all the universe. Properly spoken his title is "I am that I am." In Hebrew we would pronounce it *"Ehyeh asher Ehyeh."*

The name means that God is always present, always existing, always being whatever he needs to be for his people. It is really the precursor to all of the more than 700 names and titles for God and his Son in the entire Bible. Jesus takes on himself the name of his Father in heaven when in John 8:58 he said, *"Before Abraham was I AM"* thus making himself equal to God, the equivalent of God, and existing together with the Father from the beginning. The Jews had no doubt about his statement. They immediately picked up stones to stone him to death for this blasphemy.

Throughout the Old Testament we see the LORD transforming himself into whatever he needed to be for the people of Israel. When he would do this He would then give them a new name by which to call Him.

God is, and therefore Jesus is, able to be whatever he chooses to be whenever we need him. He is the self-existing God who can show himself as a burning bush (Our *"God is a consuming fire"*, Hebrews 12:29), or the Rock as in 1 Corinthians 10:4, *"for they all drank from the spiritual rock that accompanied them, and that Rock is Christ."*

What do you need God to be for your today, this week, this month, this year? Ask Him! He is ready to be for you whatever you need him to be. Just call on Him. He promised, *"Call upon me and I will answer you and show you great and mighty things you do not know."* (Jeremiah 33:3) and *"He is able to do exceeding abundantly above all that we ask or think, according to the power that is at work in us..."* (Eph. 3:20)

Closing Thought
The Lord is limitless in His ability to meet your need. God is able, ready and willing to be whatever you need him to be. Ask him. He is the Great I AM, to be your Healer, Helper, Provider, Protector, Sanctifier, Forgiver, Redeemer, Rescuer, Restorer, Rebuilder, Hiding Place, High Tower, Shield, Defender, Advocate, Blesser, Restorer, Supplier, Shepherd, Peace, Counselor, Righteousness, Rock, Song, Anchor, Keeper, Potter, Portion and your Inheritance. (And so much more!)

Prayer
Lord Jesus, forgive me for thinking of you as less than you are. Help me, like Thomas to fall at your feet and declare, "My Lord and my God." You are God appearing in human form, not a lesser god. You are the King of kings, and the Lord of Lords. You are all that the Father is, and I adore you and I worship you.

Discuss Together
1. In the Star Trek series there is a character described as a Shape-Shifter which was based on ancient mythology of a creature that could transform itself into any form it desired. That is really what God is implying in the "I AM that I AM" he presented to Moses.
2. If God could be anything for you today, what would you like him to be for you? Why? Can you think of him anywhere in Scripture being that for his people?
3. If you could choose only 12 names (one for each month of the year) what twelve would you chose? Why? Share your favorite names of the Lord. See our list to help you remember all of them.

Day 38
My Bridegroom

*The bride belongs to the **bridegroom**. The friend who attends the **bridegroom** waits and listens for him, and is full of joy when he hears the **bridegroom**'s voice. That joy is mine, and it is now complete.*
-- John 3:29

In our western culture today the bride gets all the attention and the groom goes fairly unnoticed. Just look around at our culture. We have "Brides" magazines but have you ever seen a magazine titled "Groom." There is even a wedding march that we traditionally call, "Here Comes the Bride." Almost everything about a western marriage is about the bride.

That is quite different from biblical times when the bridegroom was the center of attention. We tend to be a matriarchal culture while eastern cultures are patriarchal. The Bible was written by and for a patriarchal society. The man is the focus of attention. The groom is the mighty hero of the wedding ceremony. The bride, on the other hand, goes unnoticed. She is silent. She is veiled.

Even nature places the focus of attention on the male. It is the male bird that has the bright plumage, but the female is rather plain. It is the male peacock that puffs up his colorful plumage and shows off his prowess to the female. With deer it is the male deer, the buck, that gets the mighty antlers that spread his glory. This difference is quite startling to the western world view and makes it difficult for us to comprehend the "Bridegroom" talk in Scripture.

Isaiah 54:5 tells us that the Creator will become our husband (bridegroom). Jesus Christ declares himself to be the bridegroom and the church is his bride. He is to be the center of our attention. He is the honored one. He is the altogether lovely one. He is to be lifted up and exalted. He is the hero of the day. He is the focus of everyone's attention. All wait expectantly for him, and when he arrives there is a shout, there is singing and dancing. There is a triumphant processional singing, not "Here comes the Bride," but "The King is Coming!"

His arrival signals celebration. The culmination is the wedding ceremony, the marriage supper of the Lamb. He comes to rescue his bride and carry her away and keep her to himself forever.

Closing Thought

Jesus taught that he was going away with the promise that he would come again just as they saw him go. Jesus is coming to take his bride away. His bride is his pride and joy, his church, his family, his beloved one. Are you waiting expectantly for the coming of the Lord? Are you excited about his coming? Are you praying daily, "Even so, come quickly Lord Jesus"?

Prayer

Lord, I have to admit that my focus is on the here and now and not on the sweet by and by. My attention is almost entirely on my life here on earth and the struggle to just get by, to succeed in life, to have lots of stuff, and to be in good health. Teach me to love your appearing.

Discuss Together

1. Describe the most beautiful wedding you've ever seen. What was most impressive? What was the best part of the ceremony?
2. For the women: How did you feel on your wedding day as you stood at the back of the sanctuary about ready to walk into the arms of the man of your dreams? How do you think your fiancé/husband felt at that moment? That's how Christ feels about you.
3. For the men: On your wedding day you stood at an altar and your bride appeared dressed more beautifully than ever before. How did you feel when you saw her in her wedding dress and walking down the aisle toward you? That's how Jesus feels about you.

Day 39
My Jesus, Yeshua

*She shall bring forth a son, and you shall call his name **JESUS**: for he shall save his people from their sins. -- Matthew 1:21*

Heroes. There aren't very many of them left. When they do show up it is almost always in the middle of insurmountable odds and incredible difficulties.

On January 13, 1982, an Air Florida 737 crashed into the Potomac River after takeoff from Washington DC's National Airport. Only five passengers survived the terrible crash. There was a major snowstorm that was covering the Washington, D.C. area with considerable accumulation. At 3:59 p.m. an airplane took off from nearby Washington National Airport. But something was wrong with the plane. Due to wing icing and pilot error, the aircraft lost altitude and crashed into the 14th Street Bridge and the Potomac River less than a mile from the airport. It hit several cars and went into the frozen river. There were 79 people on the plane.

The plane quickly sank beneath the ice. Only its tail remained above the surface. There were six people holding onto it. "Help!" They cried. It was obvious that they could not live long in such cold water. Those six had to be saved quickly.

A police helicopter arrived at once and threw a rope to them. A woman caught it, but she was so weak that she lost her grip and fell into the water. She was about to drown. At that moment a young man, who was watching from the shore, jumped into the river. He brought her to land. Her body was so cold that she was only a few minutes from death.

But a middle-aged man was even more heroic. Identified as Arland Williams, he was among the six people on the plane's tail. The pilot of the helicopter threw a rope to him. But the man saw a young woman near him. Her face was pale and her eyes were filled with fear. He gave her the rope and helped her hold it. He wanted to save her first. When the helicopter came back, the man was still there. Again the rope was thrown to him, and again he passed it to a fellow passenger. When the helicopter finally returned to pick him up, he was nowhere in sight.

Closing Thought

Everyone loves a hero, just as everyone loves to hate the villain. It's what makes a good story and what makes the world go around. Jesus is our Hero. He is our one and only Savior. He dove into the deep waters of our sin and took on himself all the sins of the whole world that he could be our substitute and die in our place. Then he did what no other hero could do. He broke free of the bonds of death and tore open the gates of hell to triumph over death, hell and the devil that we might be saved.

Prayer

Jesus, you are my hero, but so much more than that. You are my Savior, my one and only Savior who laid down his life for me. You did that when I was still a sinner, far from God, unworthy of any help. But you loved me anyway. Thank you for that great sacrifice for me when I was not worthy the least of your favor.

Discuss Together

1. Have you ever been rescued? Have you ever been in a life or death state when someone came along and saved you? Tell your story.
2. Have you ever given up a kidney to save the life of another, or has anyone given a kidney to save your life? Tell that story. How do you feel about the one who gave so much to save your life?

Day 40
My Almighty God

*I am Alpha and Omega, the beginning and the ending, says the Lord, which is, and which was, and which is to come, the **Almighty**.*
-- Revelation 1:8

We seem to be fixated on superheroes these days. Have you noticed? Can you name them or even keep up with them? (Superman, Batman, Hulk, Captain America, Wonder Woman, Iron Man, Spiderman, etc.) This is nothing new. The ancient Greeks had a myriad of gods and goddesses that took on the form of superheroes to accomplish super human feats that mortal men can only dream about.

I suppose I will never forget the first Superman movie, "Superman, the Movie," in which Lois Lane dies in an earthquake and Superman arrives a minute too late. He explodes in anger and jumps into hyper space to encircle the earth, spinning around it counterclockwise to turn back time. He finally succeeds in turning back the clock and arriving in time to save Lois. What a superhero!

We all seem to need superheroes. They don't exist except in our minds. But ONE exists who exceeds all expectation of every superhero ever invented by man. He has given us all the Superhero we will every need.

Some people struggle with seeing Jesus as All Powerful, just like the Father. In the Old Testament God is called El Shaddai, meaning All Powerful. Yet in the New Testament Jesus takes on that persona because in him dwelt all the fullness of the Father bodily. (Colossians 2:9 and Ephesians 3:19) He and the Father are one. Jesus said, *"All power is given unto me in heaven and in earth."* (Matthew 28:18) In his earthly ministry He demonstrated his Almighty power when He raised the dead, healed every disease, cast out demons with His word, walked on water, turned water into wine, multiplied five loaves and two fish into twelve baskets full, caused a fig tree to whither with a word, and calmed storms with his command. Who is like Him? Nothing is too hard for Him. He can do immeasurably more than we ask or even imagine. His name is THE ALMIGHTY. His name is JESUS!

Closing Thought

Jesus demonstrated his power over all the forces of nature in the Gospels. Then he declared that nothing was impossible with God, and we could move mountains into the sea if we would just believe him. Then Paul affirms that *"He is able to do immeasurably more than we ask or even imagine."* What's your impossibility today? The Almighty God invites you to take His hand and allow Him to show Himself strong on your behalf.

Prayer

Lord, I admit I'm more like Thomas than Peter. At least Peter had the courage to get out of the boat and walk on water. Thomas was the doubter. I am a doubter more than a believer. I am more of a naturalist, a realist, a fatalist than a true believer. I haven't trusted in your mighty power to move the mountains I face. I tend to look for my own way of getting around the difficulties I face. Teach me to be a "believer" who trusts that you are able and willing to demonstrate your power on my behalf.

Discuss Together

1. Have you ever seen God do the impossible? A miracle or an answer to prayer? Share that story.
2. Are there things in your life that your heart believes to be impossible, even for God? Share that fear.
3. Can you bring to mind some precious promises God has given us in His word concerning his ability and willingness to help in times of trouble? Share those promises.
4. Take time to look at all the miracles Jesus did in the Gospels. Reading them and thinking about his mighty power builds faith. Faith comes by hearing and hearing by the word of God.

His Name Worship Songs

There are many more songs and hymns that exalt the name of the Lord than can be listed here. These, however, serve as a taste or a sampling of music and lyrics that are available to assist us in our worship of his glorious name. Due to copyright restrictions we are unable to list the lyrics here in this publication, but they are readily available on the Internet through use of any search engine.

The Name / Title	Suggested Song or Hymn, search on YouTube.com
1. Abba	Abba, Father, Hillsong & Steve Fry
2. Advocate	Before the Throne of God, Charitie Lees
3. All in All	You Are My All in All, Dennis L. Jernigan
4. Alpha & Omega	Prince of Peace, Marc Imboden & Tammi Rhoton
5. Altar	Is Your All of the Altar?, E.A. Hoffman
6. Amen	Handel's Messiah, Part 3: Amen
7. Anchor	My Anchor Holds, William C. Martin
8. Author	I Fix My Eyes on You, Tommy Walker
9. Beginning/Ending	He Knows My Name, Tommy Walker
10. Bread	Guide Me O Thou Great Jehovah, William William
11. Deliverer	It is Well, Horatio G. Spafford
12. Door Way	One Door, public domain
13. Friend	Friend of God, Israel Houghton and Michael Gungor
14. Gift	Behold What Manner of Love, Patricia Van Tine
15. Lamb	Lamb of Glory, Phill McHugh
16. Resurrection	Breathe on Me Breath of God, Edwin Hatch
17. Life	New Life in Christ, John W. Peterson
18. Light	The Light of the World is Jesus, P.P. Bliss
19. Lion	The Lion of Judah, by Bob Marley
20. Morning Star	The Potter's Hand, Darlene Zschech
21. Physician	Only Believe, Paul Rader
22. Protector	Day by Day, A.L. Skoog and Carolina Sandell
23. Rabboni	Spirit of God, Descend Upon, George Croly
24. Serpent	Victory in Jesus, E.M. Bartlett
25. Shepherd	Shepherd of Love, by John W. Peterson
26. Truth	Thy Word, by Amy Grant & Michael W. Smith
27. Way	My Lord Knows the Way, Sidney E. Cox
28. Wing	Under His Wings, M. Cushing
29. Sanctifier	Refiner's Fire, Brian Doerksen
30. Finisher	He's Still Working on Me, Joel Hemphill
31. Vine	Vine and Branches, Trevor Thompson,
32. Judge	Mighty to Save, Laura Story
33. Word	Thy Word, Amy Grant, Michael Card
34. Provider	No Sweeter Name, Kari Jobe
35. Potter	The Potter's Hand, Darlene Zschech
36. Ransom	Jesus Messiah, Chris Tomlin
37. I Am	The God of Abraham Praise, Daniel ben Judah
38. Bridegroom	The King is Coming, Gill Gaither
39. Jesus	The Champion of Love, Phil & Carolyn Cross
40. Almighty God	How Great Thou Art, Carl Boberg

So What? What Now?

I always try to close my sermon preparation with the most important part of that preparation, the practical application. I ask myself, "So what? What now?" In other words, "What am I supposed to do with this information and inspiration?" James 1:22 exhorts us to *"Be doers of the word and not hearers only."* So, what are we supposed to do with the Names of the Lord? And how can we be "doers" of the Name? Let me offer a couple of practical suggestions.

1. **Study His Names Together** – Malachi 3:16 says the Lord listens and takes notes on our conversations when we talk together about his name. He even writes a book of remembrance concerning us when we do this and finally, he promises significant rewards for those who do. We have provided questions as a guide to group study and discussions. These devotional thoughts can easily serve as three 10 to 13-week topical studies for small groups.

2. **Adopt a Name** – David had some favorite names of the Lord that he often referred to, as in Psalm 18:1-2. Over the years our church family has chosen one name each year to cling to, and often pray to, the Lord using that name. It is a wonderful way to make the name of the Lord more than just a name. There is power in the Name of the Lord. That power is activated by faith. Believing and trusting in what God has promised he would be for us is a life enriching experience. What name is God impressing on you to embrace? Consider adopting one name for each month of the coming year.

3. **Bear, Wear, and Share His Name** – As believers we are people of the Name. We are to bear his name to others and testify of his greatness, goodness and grace. Wearing a pendant, wristband, necklace, bracelet or some other visible reminder of the Name can be a wonderful opportunity to share with others the significance of the Lord's name to you. In Deuteronomy 6:4-9, God encourages his people to write down his word, his commandments, and wear them to be reminded constantly of his word. We can do the same with the Names of the Lord, whether it is a t-shirt, a piece of jewelry, a poster on the wall, or a magnet on your refrigerator, these visible emblems of his Name call the attention of our friends and colleagues to let them know that we love the Lord in first place.

Celebrate the Name of Jesus
A Christian Christmas Tree

One of the most delightful and anticipated worship services of the year in our church has been the Chrismon Service. Each year I preach a series of five or six Advent messages proclaiming and expounding on one of the many names of the Lord.

At the end of that series we conduct an evening Christmas Service in which the Names of the Lord are lifted up in song, Scriptures, and through decorating the Christmas tree with ornaments that declare the name of the Lord. We encourage everyone to participate and to go forward to the Christmas tree to worship Christ for his exalted name, taking with them one of their favorite names of the Lord.

The service is a visual reminder and a tool for helping young and old identify the wondrous names of Jesus, and to consider the real identity of the baby in the manger. It also encourages each believer to trust in the Name of the Lord, and embrace his name as their own special name of Christ for the coming year.

Making your own ornaments can be a worthwhile exercise in reviewing and rejoicing in the *Name Above All Names*. We suggest you keep it simple, yet attractive with just the name of the Lord. There is no need to try to replicate any of the images or even print the verse or text. Simple red or white ornaments are best.

A Chrismon Service

Malachi 3:16

*"Then they that feared the Lord spoke often one with another;
and the Lord hearkened and heard it, and a book of remembrance was written
before him for them that feared the Lord and that thought on his name."*

*Praise the LORD. Praise, O servants of the LORD, praise the name of the
LORD. 2 Blessed be the name of the LORD from this time forth and for
evermore. 3 From the rising of the sun unto the going down of the same the
LORD'S name is to be praised. – Psalm 113:1-3*

It is our prayer that through this service Jesus Christ will be so lifted up,
exalted and glorified that men will be drawn to him, bow before him, and
worship him as Savior and Lord. Gloria Excelsis Deo.

Prelude

Welcome and Opening Words
  Opening Worship Set - The Name of the Lord
  Songs: Prince of Peace, Forever, All Hail the Power, Friend of Sinners

Explanation of the Service
  Prayer
  Giving our Offerings to Jesus

Chrismon Service:
Scripture reading of the listed passages followed by the singing of a
hymn while those emblems are placed on the tree.

Creation Names - Ps 139:1-9, Hebrews 1:1-3, John 1:1-3
Songs: The Name of the Lord Is, Angels We Have Heard

Strong Names - Exodus 15:1-13, Ex 33:9-11, 14-15, 18-23, Ex 34:5-8
Songs: O Come All Ye Faithful, Emmanuel, Praise the Name of Jesus

Eternal Names - Philippians 2:5-11, Revelation 1:11-18
Songs: Joy to the World, Ancient of Days, Holy and Anointed One

Savior Names - Mt 1:18-21, Revelation 19:1-17 (11-17)
Songs: Hark! The Herald Angels, Jesus Name Above All Names

Closing: O Holy Night (acappella)

All lights will be extinguished except tree lights. As you enter this evening you
were offered a "Chrismon" to use in decorating the Christ-tree. After the pastor
reads the meaning of that emblem, and during the song that follows, you may
approach the tree with other having the same emblem and decorate the tree.
Make this a time of worship as you would honor the birth of the King.

Emblems of His Name
Make It <u>His</u> Tree Again

Who his own self bare our sins in his own body on the <u>tree</u>,
that we, being dead to sins, should live unto righteousness:
by whose stripes you were healed. - 1 Peter 2:24

A tree has great symbolism and the Christmas tree has long been the instrument for exalting Christ at Christmas. Martin Luther originated the Christianizing of the Yule tree when he gave symbolic meaning to each item on the tree.

Why not make it a family tradition to adopt a name of the Lord for every year and place an ornament on the tree to exalt his name together?

Check more Christ exalting emblems available at <u>www.PrayerToday.org</u>.

52 Weeks with the Name of Jesus

The Names of the Lord seem to be a limitless bounty for discovering the character and person of God himself. I have been studying and categorizing those names for forty years and I have compiled over 700 separate names and titles for the Lord. May the Lord himself give you encouragement as you discover, meditate and embrace his Names and Titles.

(Week 1) Animal Names
1. Lion of Judah - Rev. 5:5
2. Fiery Serpent - Numbers 21:4-9, John 3:14
3. Lamb of God - John 1:29
4. Scapegoat - Leviticus 16:5
5. Mother Hen/Eagle - Matthew 23:37, Dt 32:11
6. Eagle Wings - Exodus 19:4, Isa. 40:30-31
7. Dove - Mattehw 3:16 , John 1:32-34

(Week 2) Strong Names
1. I AM - Exodus 3:14
2. Consuming Fire - Deuteronomy 4:24
3. Almighty God - Genesis 17:1
4. Everlasting Father - Isaiah 9:6
5. Mighty God - Isaiah 9:6
6. Rock - Psalm 18:2
7. Strength - Psalm 18:2

(Week 3) Jehovah Names
1. Jehovah-Jireh - Genesis 22:14
2. Jehovah-Shalom - Judges 6:24
3. Jehovah-Rapha - Exodus 15:26
4. Jehovah-Rohi - Psalm 23:1
5. Jehovah-Nissi - Exodus 17:15
6. Jehovah-Shammah -Ezekiel 48:35
7. Jehovah-M'Kaddesh - Leviticus 20:8

(Week 4) Ministry Names
1. Potter - Isaiah 64:8, Jeremiah 18:6
2. Restorer - Psalm 23:3, Joel 2:25
3. Refiner - Malachi 3:2-3
4. Rebuilder – Is. 54:11, 58:12, Rev. 21:5
5. Redeemer - 1 Sam. 6:20, Job 19:25
6. Counselor - Isaiah 9:6
7. Apostle - Hebrews 3:1

(Week 5) Military Names
1. Lord of Hosts- Psalm 24:10
2. Sword - Deuteronomy 33:29, Joshua 7:18
3. Shield - Psalms 28:7, Ps. 119:114, Ps. 144:2
4. Fortress - Psalm 18:2
5. High Tower - Psalm 18:2
6. Horn of Salvation - Psalm 18:2
7. Rearguard - Isaiah 52:12, Isaiah 58:8

(Week 6) Beauty Names
1. Lily of the Valley - Song of Solomon 2:1
2. Bright Morning Star - Revelation 22:16
3. Rose of Sharon - Song of Solomon 2:1
4. Altogether Lovely - Song of Solomon 5:16
5. Wonderful - Isaiah 9:6
6. Brightness of His Glory - Hebrews 1:3
7. Pearl of Greatest Price – Matt. 13:46

(Week 7) Illustrative Names
1. Altar - Hebrews 13:10
2. Anchor - Hebrews 6:19
3. Banner - Song of Solomon 2:4, Ex. 17:15
4. Cup - Psalm 16:5
5. Hiding Place - Psalm 32:7
6. Cornerstone - Is. 28:16, Eph 2:20, 1 Pet. 2:6
7. Resting Place - Jeremiah 50:6

(Week 8) Object Names
1. Word - John 1:1
2. Bread - John 6:48
3. Door - John 10:9
4. Way - John 14:6
5. Vine - John 15:1
6. Light of World - John 1:9, John 8:12
7. Good Shepherd - John 10:11, 14

(Week 9) Position Names
1. Great Shepherd - Hebrews 13:20
2. Captain - Hebrews 2:10
3. Bishop - 1 Peter 2:25
4. Bridegroom - John 3:29
5. Counselor - Isaiah 9:6
6. King of Kings - 1 Tim. 6:15, Rev. 19:16
7. Author - Hebrews 5:9, Hebrews 12:2

(Week 10) Gracious Names
1. My Shade - Psalms 121:5
2. My Goodness - Psalm 144:2
3. My Glory - Psalms 3:3
4. The Lifter of Head - Psalms 3:3
5. My Keeper - Psalm 121:5
6. My Song - Isaiah 12:2, Exodus 15:2
7. My Salvation - Exodus 15:2

(Week 11) Rich Names
1. Indescribable Gift - 2 Corinthians 9:15
2. Ransom for Many – Matt. 20:28, 1 Tim.2:6
3. Reward/Rewarder - Rev. 22:12, Hebrews 11:6
4. Portion - Psalm 73:26, Lamentations 3:24
5. Inheritance - Psalm 16:5
6. Strength – Ex. 15:2, 2 Sam.22:33, Ps 28:7
7. Diadem of Beauty - Isaiah 28:5

(Week 12) Nature Names
1. Water of Life - John 7:38, Psalm 143:6
2. Refuge - Psalm 59:16
3. Fountain of Living Water - Jeremiah 17:13
4. Pavilion - Psalm 31:20
5. Shelter - Psalm 61:3
6. Well of Water - John 4:14, 1 Cor. 10:4
7. Sun of Righteousness - Malachi 4:2

(Week 13) Hero Names
1. Deliverer - Psalm 40:17
2. Defense - Psalm 94:22
3. Strength - Isaiah 12:2, Psalm 27:1
4. Prince of Peace - Isaiah 9:6
5. Judge - Genesis 18:25, Jud. 11:27, Acts 10:42
6. Victor - Psalms 98:1, 1 Corinthians 15:57
7. Very Present Help - Psalm 46:1

(Week 14) Deity Names
1. Alpha & Omega - Revelation 1:8
2. First & Last - Revelation 1:11, 17, 2:8: 22:13
3. Beginning & Ending – Rev. 1:8, 21:6, 22:13
4. Living One - Revelation 1:18, Revelation 2:8
5. Emmanuel - Isaiah 7:14, Matthew 1:23
6. Coming King - Rev 3:11, Rev. 22:7, 12, 20
7. Holder of Keys - Revelation 1:18

Week 15) Kingly Names
1. Anointed One - 1 Sam. 2:35, Psalm 23:5
2. Scepter - Numbers 24:17
3. King of Kings - 1 Tim. 6:15, Rev. 17:14, 19:16
4. Lord of Lords - 1 Tim. 6:15, Rev. 17:14, 19:16
5. Ruler - Micah 5:2
6. King Eternal - 1 Timothy 1:17
7. Prince of Life - Acts 3:15

(Week 16) Priestly Names
1. High Priest - Hebrews 5:5, 6:20
2. Intercessor - Isaiah 53:12, Hebrews 7:25
3. Mediator - Hebrews 8:6
4. Minister of Sanctuary -
5. Offering for Sin - Isaiah 53:10
6. Man of Sorrows - Isaiah 53:3
7. Justifier - Isaiah 53:11, Rom. 3:24, 5:9, 8:33

(Week 17) Medical Names
1. Healer - Exodus 15:26
2. Health of my Countenance - Psalm 43:5
3. Balm in Gilead - Jeremiah 8:22
4. Great Physician - Jeremiah 8:22, Luke 5:31
5. Branch - Exodus 15:25, Jeremiah 23:5
6. Anointer with Oil - Psalm 45:7, Is. 61:1
7. Healer with Stripes - Isaiah 53:5

(Week 18) Christmas Names
1. Holy Child - Acts 4:27
2. Carpenter's Son - Matthew 13:55, Mark 6:3
3. Son of God - Mark 1:1
4. Jesus of Nazareth - Matthew 21:11, 26:71
5. Star of Jacob - Numbers 24:17
6. Only Begotten Son - John 1:14, John 3:16
7. Tender Plant - Isaiah 53:1

(Week 19) Superlative Names
1. Immortal - 1 Timothy 1:17
2. Invisible -1 Timothy 1:17
3. Only Wise God - 1 Timothy 1:17
4. Maker of All Things - Hebrews 1:2, John 1:3
5. Image of God - 2 Corinthians 4:4
6. Brightness of His Glory - Hebrews 1:3
7. Express Image of Person - Hebrews 1:3

(Week 20) Miscellaneous Names
1. All in All - Colossians 3:11
2. Amen - Revelation 3:14
3. Day Star - 2 Peter 1:19
4. Omniscient One - Isaiah 40:13
5. Omnipresent One - Isaiah 41:10
6. Heir of All Things - Hebrews 1:2
7. Guide Even Unto Death - Psalm 48:14

(Week 21) Extra Names
1. Resurrection - John 11:25
2. Life - John 11:25, John 1:4
3. Truth - John 14:6
4. Faithful - Revelation 19:11
5. Friend of Sinners – Matt. 11:19, Luke 7:34
6. First Born - Colossians 1:15, 18
7. Rabbi - John 1:38

(Week 21) Extra Names
1. Passover - 1 Corinthians 5:7
2. Pearl of Great Price - Mat 13:45-46
3. Friend of Sinners - Matt. 11:19, Luke 7:34
4. First Born - Colossians 1:15, 18
5. Guide Even Unto Death - Psalms 48:14
6. Health of my countenance - Psalms 43:5
7. Revealer of Secrets – Daniel 2:47

(Week 22) "El" Names (Character of God)
1. El Shaddai - All-Sufficient - Gen. 17:1
2. El De'ot - All Knowing - 1 Sam 2:3
3. El Channun - All Gracious - Jonah 4:2
4. El Erekh Apayim - All Patient - (Rom 15:5
5. El Rachum - All Compassion - Deut 4:31
6. El malei Rachamim - All Merciful - Dt 4:31
7. El Selichot - All Forgiving - Neh 9:17

(Week 23) "El" Names (God's Lordship)
1. El Gibbor - Mighty God - (Champion) Isa. 9:6
2. El Haggadol - Great God - Deut. 10:17
3. El Hakkavod - God of Glory - Ps. 29:3
4. El Hakkadosh - Holy God - Isa. 5:16
5. El Hashamayim - of Heavens - Ps. 136:26
6. El Mishpat - God of Justice - Isaiah 30:18
7. El-Channun - Gracious God - Jonah 4:2

(Week 24) "El" Names (My Personal God)
1. El Ro'i - God Who Sees (me) - Gen. 16:13
2. El Chaiyai - God of my Life - Ps. 42:8
3. El Yeshuatenu - God of Deliverance - Ps 68:19
4. El Tehilati - God of My Praise - Psalm 109:1
5. El Hannora - Awesome God - Neh. 9:32
6. El Mauzi - God of my Strength - Psalm 43:2
7. El Chaiyai - God of my Life - Ps. 42:8

(Week 26) Jehovah Names (My Help)
1. Jehovah - The Lord - Exodus 6:2, 3
2. Jehovah 'Immeku- Lord with you - Judges 6:12
3. Jehovah 'Ez Lami - Lord My Strength - Ps 28:7
4. Jehovah 'Ori - Lord My Light - Psalm 27:1
5. Jehovah Adonai - Lord God - Genesis 15:2
6. Jehovah Bara - Lord Creator - Isaiah 40:28
7. Jehovah Chereb - Lord my Sword - Deut. 33:29

(Week 27) Jehovah Names (My God)
1. Jehovah Eli - Lord My God (Psalm 18:2
2. Jehovah Elyon - Lord Most High (Psalm 38:2
3. Jehovah Ganan - Lord Defense - Psalm 89:18
4. Jehovah Go'el - Lord Redeemer – Isa. 49:26
5. Jehovah Hamelech - Lord the King - Psalm 98:6
6. Jehovah Hashopet – Lord the Judge - Jud. 6:27
7. Jehovah Helech 'Olam - King Forever - Ps10:16

(Week 28) Jehovah Names (My Warrior King)
1. Jehovah Gador Milchamah - Mighty Warrior Ps 24:8
2. Jehovah Keren Yish'l - Horn of Salvation - Ps 18:2
3. Jehovah Ma'oz - My Fortress - Jer. 16:19
4. Jehovah Machsi - My Refuge - Ps 91:9
5. Jehovah Magen - My Shield - Deut. 33:29
6. Jehovah Misqabbi - My High Tower – Ps 18:2
7. Jehovah Mephalti - Lord My Deliverer - Ps18:2

(Week 29) Jehovah Names (My Perfecter)
1. Jehovah Kabodhi - Lord my Glory - Psalm 3:3
2. Jehovah M'Kaddesh - Sanctifier - I Cor.1:30
3. Jehovah Melech Olam - King Forever - Ps 10:16
4. Jehovah Naheh - Lord who Smites - Ezekiel 7:9
5. Jehovah Sel'I - Lord My Rock - Psalm 18:2
6. Jehovah Tsori - Lord My Strength - Psalm 19:14
7. Jehovah Yasha - Lord Our Savior - Isa. 49:26

(Week 30) Gospel of John
1. Lord - John 1:23
2. Rabbi - John 1:38
3. Master - John 1:38
4. Jesus of Nazareth - John 1:45
5. King of Israel - John 1:49
6. Teacher from God - John 3:2
7. Son of Man - John 3:13

(Week 31) Gospel of John
1. Creator - John 1:3
2. Son of God - John 1:34
3. King - John 1:49
4. Lamb of God - John 1:29
5. Light - John 1:9
6. Truth - John 14:6
7. Life - John 14:6

(Week 32) Gospel of John
1. Gift of God (John 4:10)
2. Savior of the world (John 4:42)
3. I AM (John 8:58)
4. Son of Joseph (John 6:42)
5. The Man (John 19:5)
6. Prophet (John 7:40)
7. King of the Jews (John 18:33)

(Week 33) Gospel of John
1. Rabboni (John 20:16)
2. Lord and God (John 20:28)
3. Resurrection (John 11:25)
4. Comforter - John 14:16-18
5. Gift of God - John 4:10
6. Lord and God – John 21:28
7. Advocate - 1 John 2:1

(Week 34) Revelation
1. Faithful and True (Rev. 19:11)
2. Faithful Witness (Rev. 1:5)
3. Faithful and True Witness (Rev. 3:14)
4. First Love (Rev 2:4)
5. First and Last (Rev. 1:17; 2:8; 22:13)
6. Firstborn from the Dead (Rev. 1:5)
7. God of the Prophets (Rev 22:6)

(Week 35) Revelation
1. Holder of the Keys (Rev 1:18)
2. Holder of Sharp 2-Edged Sword (Rev 2:12)
3. Holy and True (Rev. 3:7)
4. King of the Ages (Rev 15:3)
5. Living One (Rev. 1:18)
6. Lord of Lords (Rev 17:14)
7. Offspring of David (Rev. 22:16)

(Week 36) Revelation
1. Root of David (Rev. 5:5)
2. Ruler of Creation (Rev. 3:14)
3. Ruler of Kings (Rev. 1:5)
4. Who Was, Is, and Is to Come (Rev. 1:4)
5. Worthy Lamb – Rev. 5:12
6. Jesus Christ – Rev. 1:1
7. Coming Kind – Rev. 22:12

(Week 37) Hebrews
1. The Only Begotten Son - Heb. 1:2, 1:5, 5:5
2. Heir of All Things - Heb. 1:2
3. Maker of Worlds - Heb. 1:2
4. Brightness of God's Glory - Heb. 1:3
5. Exact Image of God's Person - Heb. 1:3
6. Upholder of All Things - Heb. 1:3
7. Purger of Sins - Heb. 1:3

(Week 38) Hebrews
1. Majestic Enthroned Savior - Heb. 1:3
2. The Most Excellent Name - Heb. 1:4
3. The One Worshiped by Angels - Heb. 1:6
4. The Eternal Changeless One - Heb. 1:12
5. Taster of Death for every man - Heb. 2:9
6. Captain of our Salvation - Heb. 2:10
7. Victor over Death and Devil - Heb. 2:14

(Week 39) Hebrews
1. Destroyer of Death and Devil - Heb. 2:14
2. Deliverer from the fear of Death - Heb. 2:15
3. Merciful High Priest - Heb. 2:17
4. Faithful High Priest - Heb. 2:17
5. Sympathizing High Priest - Heb. 2:18, 4:15
6. High Priest of our Profession - Heb. 3:1
7. Son over his Own House - Heb. 3:6

(Week 40) Hebrews
1. Apostle of our Profession - Heb. 3:1
2. All-Seeing One - Heb. 4:13
3. Great High Priest - Heb. 4:14
4. Penetrator of Hearts - Heb. 4:12
5. The Word of God/Sword - Heb. 4:12
6. Touched with our Infirmities - Heb. 4:15
7. Forever High Priest - Heb. 5:6, 6:20, 7:17, 7:21,

(Week 41) Hebrews
1. Forerunner - Heb. 6:20
2. Anchor of the Soul - Heb. 6:19
3. Our Intercessor - Heb. 7:25
4. Minister of the Sanctuary - Heb. 8:2
5. Mediator - Heb. 8:6, 9:15, 12:24
6. Intercessor - Heb. 8:25-26
7. Coming King - Heb. 10:37

(Week 42) Hebrews
1. Author of Eternal Salvation - Heb 5:9
2. Author of our Faith - Heb 12:2
3. Finisher of our Faith - Heb 12:2
4. Consuming Fire - Heb 12:29
5. Our Helper - Heb 13:6
6. The Same, Yest., Today, Forever - Heb 13:8
7. Great Shepherd - Heb 13:20

(Week 43) Isaiah
1. Banner - Isa. 11:10
2. Beautiful Wreath - Isa. 28:6
3. Branch of the Lord - Isa. 4:2, 11:1
4. Consuming Fire - Isa. 33:14
5. Creator - Isa. 40:28
6. Everlasting God - Isa. 40:28
7. Israel's Creator - Isa. 43:15

(Week 44) Isaiah
1. First and Last - Isa. 41:4, 44:6, 48:12
2. Fortress - Isa. 17:10
3. Glorious Crown - Isa. 28:5
4. Glorious Presence - Isa. 3:8, 4:5-6
5. God Your Savior - Isa. 17:10
6. God of the Whole Earth - Isa. 54:5
7. Holy God - Isa. 5:16

(Week 46) Isaiah
1. Holy One of Israel - Isa. 1:4, 5:24
2. Husband - Isa. 54:5
3. I Am God - Isa. 43:12
4. I Am He - Isa. 43:13
5. I Am the Lord - Isa. 43:15, 44:24
6. Immanuel - Isa. 7:14

(Week 47) Isaiah
1. Judge - Isa. 33:22
2. King - Isa. 6:5, 33:22
3. King in his Beauty - Isa. 33:17
4. Law Giver - Isa. 33:22
5. Light of Israel - Isa. 10:17
6. Lord Almighty 1:9
7. Lord - Isa. 1:2

(Week 48) Isaiah
1. Maker - Isa. 45:9, 11
2. Mighty One of Israel - Isa. 1:24, 30:29
3. Mighty One of Jacob - Isa. 49:26, 60:16
4. One who made it all - Isa. 22:11
5. Our Mighty One - Isa. 33:21
6. Rear Guard - Isa. 52:12
7. Way in the Wilderness - Isa. 43:19

(Week 49) Isaiah
1. Redeemer - Isa. 41:4, 44:24
2. Righteous One - Isa. 24:16
3. Rock of Israel - Isa. 30:29
4. Rock - Isa. 17:10
5. Root of Jesse - Isa. 11:10
6. Savior Alone - Isa. 43:11
7. Savior of Israel - Isa. 45:15

(Week 50) Isaiah
1. Shade from Heat - Isa. 25:4
2. Shelter in Storm - Isa. 25:4
3. Shepherd - Isa. 40:11
4. Source of Strength - Isa. 28:6
5. Sovereign Lord - Isa. 50:4
6. Upright One - Isa. 26:7
7. Your Holy One - Isa.43:15

(Week 51) Miscellaneous
1. Unspeakable Gift - 2 Corinthians 9:15
2. Wall of Fire - Zechariah 2:5
3. Glory Within - Zechariah 2:5
4. My Support - Psalm 18:18
5. Rescuer – Psalm 18:17, 19
6. Revealer of Secrets – Daniel 2:47
7. God of all Gods – Daniel 2:47

(Week 52) He's the Seven-Way King
1. King of Israel - John 12:13
2. King of Righteousness - Hebrews 7:2
3. King of the Ages - Rev. 15:3
4. King of Heaven - Daniel 4:37
5. King of Glory - Psalms 24:7
6. King of kings - 1 Timothy 6:15
7. King of the Jews - Matthew 2:2

Extra Names
- Avenger – Psalm 94:1
- Provider – Psalm 34:8-10, 104:27
- Protector – Psalm 5:11, Ps 20:1
- Holy Spirit (Ruach Qodesh) – Ps 51:11, Is 63:10
- Father to Fatherless – Psalm 68:5
- Defender of Widows – Psalm 68:5
- Desert Owl (Messianic) Psalm 102:6
- Their Glory – Psalm 106:20
- One Enthroned on High – Ps 113:5
- Preserver of Life – Psalm 119:88
- He Who Watches Over You – Psalm 121:3-8
- My Loving God – Psalm 144:2
- Victory Giver – Psalm 144:10
- Blesser – Psalm 115:12, Num. 6:24, Is 30:
- Rock that is Higher than I - Psalms 61:2
- Shadow of the Almighty - Psalms 91:1
- Spirit (Ruach) – Num. 11:1-25, 27:18, Jdg 3:10
- Faithful God – Deut. 7:9

Other Books by Richard W. LaFountain
"Developing Intimacy with God"

"Spending Time Alone With God" is the first of Pastor Dick's books on prayer and intimacy with God. It's the story of his own struggle to pray and stay in the presence of God without getting bored and sleepy. God led him to a prayer pattern that has been effective in his own prayer journey and has proved useful to many others over the last 25 years. Now it is available to you too. It's more than a book. It's more like a training manual with disciplines to work at in your own prayer life. It will transform the way your pray!

"3-Minutes Alone with God" is a follow-up to "*Spending Time Alone With God.*" It gives you helps and tools for your prayer life that will make praying more enjoyable and exciting. Included in this book is a workbook to help you develop prayer skills. The workbook portion is also available online is an 8 ½ x 11 format, ideal for printing your own copies. It is free of charge.

These books and other prayer products are available only at www.PrayerToday.org and www.MinistryToday.org.

Blessed be the Name
A 40-Day Devotion on Old Testament Names of God

There are over 700 Names of the Lord in Scripture so that we might know and experience God in all his love and glory.

Available at www.PrayerToday.org

Watch our web site for new articles, updates and new helps and products to assist your walk with Christ. www.PrayerToday.org